THE RUSKINS IN NO.

By the same author

John Ruskin, *The Stones of Venice*, abridged
and edited by J. G. Links, Collins, 1960
Venice for Pleasure The Bodley Head, 1966
Venice (Portraits of Cities) Lutterworth Press, 1967

The Ruskins in Normandy

*A Tour in 1848 with
Murray's Hand-book*

J. G. LINKS

JOHN MURRAY

© J. G. Links 1968

Printed in Great Britain for
John Murray, Albemarle Street, London
by William Clowes and Sons, Limited
London and Beccles
7195 1817 2

CONTENTS

ILLUSTRATIONS

Illustrations

ACKNOWLEDGMENTS

Acknowledgment and thanks are due for permission to publish letters and drawings, to the Trustees of the Pierpont Morgan Library, New York; Yale University Library; The Educational Trust Ltd., Bembridge, Isle of Wight; the Fogg Art Museum, Harvard University; Mr Frank T. Sabin, and Sir Ralph Millais, Bt. The author also desires to record his deep appreciation of help rendered by Mr James S. Dearden of the Ruskin Galleries, Bembridge; Monsieur M. d'Ymouville, Archivist of Caen; Monsieur André Dupont of Saint-Lo; Madame Elisabeth Chirol of Rouen and Monsieur I. Macary of Falaise.

Permission to quote from unpublished Ruskin material has been kindly granted by Messrs. George Allen and Unwin Ltd., John Ruskin's Literary Trustees.

TRAVEL BEFORE MURRAY

'It is just over 30 years this 1848 since I slept in a friend's house,' wrote John James Ruskin, apologising for not staying with the family of his son's bride, Effie, for their Perth wedding. He added, 'I take my ease at an Inn continually'.[1]

It was an understatement; Mr Ruskin was constantly travelling round the country building up his prosperous business as sherry merchant and since 1832 he had undertaken a long continental tour with his family almost every other year. Few families could have stayed in so many different inns—but whether they took ease in them is another matter; they seldom stayed more than one night at any one place on the road. Neither Mr nor Mrs Ruskin was young—John James Ruskin was born in 1785 and his wife in 1781—and, unlike their son, they did not travel to get to the high mountains or to study the Gothic cathedrals. 'He did not like the snow or wooden-walled rooms,' John Ruskin recalled of his father fifty years later and, as for cathedrals, Mr Ruskin had written from Salisbury to a friend in 1848, 'My son occupies himself with the architecture of the Cathedral, a lovely edifice, but I find it very slow'.[2]

The Ruskins travelled because they loved travelling for its own sake (as well, of course, as to be with their son) and when John Ruskin, as an old man, wrote his autobiography, *Praeterita,* he remembered affectionately many details of those early tours. It was not unusual, he recalled, for them to last six months and 'they began with the choice of a suitable carriage from Mr Hopkinson's of Long Acre. Then came the arranging of the carriage, the cunning design and distribution of store-cellars under the seats, secret drawers under front windows, invisible pockets under padded lining, safe from dust, and accessible only by insidious slits, the fitting of cushions where they would not slip, the rounding of corners for more delicate repose, the prudent attachments and springs of blinds . . . the little apartment was to be virtually one's home for six months and the very arranging of it was an imaginary journey in itself, with every pleasure, and none of the discomfort of practical travelling.' [3]

During those early journeys there were generally six of them in the carriage; Mr and Mrs Ruskin and John, John's nurse, Anne, and a relation or another servant (the relation sometimes acting as the servant) and a courier. The courier was essential as none of them spoke any foreign language with fluency. 'He made all the bargains and paid all the bills and knew which inns were the best and which rooms in them. He also knew the proper sights to be seen and the means to be used for getting sight of those that weren't to be seen by the vulgar.' Travel books were few and out of date and guide-books, or hand-books as they came to be known later, did not then exist.

The aristocratic traveller was used to sending his courier to ride in advance of his own carriage, ordering the horses at each post-house to be harnessed and ready waiting and so save time. Mr Ruskin would have considered it 'a trespass on the privileges of the nobility if he had taken such a course, besides involving the cost of an extra horse'. Their courier, therefore, travelled behind in the dickey with the nurse, Anne. Mr Ruskin was sensitive to his position as a man of trade and, although he liked and was willing to pay for large clean rooms on the first floor front of the best inn, he preferred not to have the best room of all. That, in his opinion, should be reserved for the nobility and he would have been embarrassed to find himself in a better room than that occupied by one of higher rank than himself— possibly one of his own customers.

A carriage of this size needed four horses to get any sufficient way on it, and half a dozen such teams were kept at every post-house. The French horses were well up to their work (although 'good-humouredly licentious' Ruskin archly remarked later) and were driven by one postillion riding the shaft horse. This was generally 'a young man, rarely drunk, half his weight being in his boots which were brought out slung from the saddle like two buckets, the postillion, after the horses were harnessed, walking along the pole and getting into them.' Then they were off, generally at nine, and on until three when they had done their day's journey of forty or fifty miles, but some days starting at six and doing twenty miles before breakfast.

GEORGE

Soon the courier was dispensed with on these tours, Mr Ruskin having learnt how to handle the courier's work himself. Instead, John Ruskin's own servant went in the party, first the 'good, honest, uninteresting Thomas Hughes', followed, in 1841, by John Hobbs, a 'sensible and merry-minded youth' of seventeen who stayed in Ruskin's service for eleven years. As Ruskin and his father were both Johns, Hobbs was rechristened George. He was kept fully occupied.

'John has been so waited on all his life', wrote Effie in 1851, 'that he requires almost one man to himself to run his errands, keep his clothes clean and all his things in order',[4] but George had more to do than this as time went on. Although the younger brother of Mrs Ruskin's maid, he was more a secretary than a valet to Ruskin. He copied out all his manuscripts in his meticulous copper-plate hand and it was George's copies, not Ruskin's, that went to the printer. When Ruskin wanted a rubbing of a piece of sculpture, George made it and when there were daguerreotypes to be taken, George took them. Ruskin describes him 'indefatigably carrying his little daguerreotype box up every where and taking the first image of the Matterhorn, as also of the Aiguilles of Chamonix, drawn by the sun. A thing to be proud of still', he rightly added.

And George kept a diary. This only recently became known when the Pierpont Morgan Library acquired a 245-page manuscript book recording in detail the Ruskins' continental tours of 1846 and 1849. This fills in many gaps left by Ruskin himself and throws fresh light on the arduous nature of the tours.

Consider, for example, that of 1846. Mr Ruskin was sixty-one and Mrs Ruskin sixty-five. Ruskin later described the 'nine to three' days, when they breakfasted at eight 'and the horses were pawing and neighing at the door (under the archway, I should have said) by nine'. Seven miles an hour, forty or fifty miles of journey, were the rule and then they 'sate down to dinner at four—and I had done two hours of delicious exploring by myself in the evening; ordered in punctually at seven to tea, and finishing my sketches till half-past nine, bed-time'.

But there were also the days, such as the first day of the 1846 tour, when they left Calais at seven in the morning and travelled nearly ninety miles to Abbeville, arriving at six-thirty in the evening. Or as when, a few days later, they drove the fifty-two miles from Beauvais to the centre of Paris, practically all on what George caustically described as 'the celebrated pavé', failed to get into any hotel in Paris and drove on, still on pavé, to Melun, twenty-seven miles south of Paris. 'However, by this affair,' George added, 'I saw more of Paris, of the streets, than if I had stopped a month.' He, too, was an inveterate sightseer.

They were away for six months and three days during which they slept in seventy-nine different beds, in fifty-one of them for but a single night. It took them three weeks to reach Venice and then, after two weeks there, they went on to Florence. Three weeks in Florence and on to Sestri Levante for a week. Over the Mont Cenis Pass and ten days at St Michel in the Cenis Plain. Then, apart from nine days in Vevey and five each in Chamonix and Lucerne, back home stopping only one night in each of the thirty-eight places they visited. They covered 2,687 miles in all.

The only regular exception to the one-night stand was Sunday. They never travelled on Sunday and, if they could reach a 'pleasant cathedral town' to spend it in, they were willing to make Saturday an exceptionally long day. Nor did Ruskin ever climb or sketch on a Sunday. He made his first Sunday climb, with George, on his first tour without his parents in 1845 and wrote in *Praeterita* that 'it remains a weight on my conscience to this day.' He made his first Sunday sketch thirteen years later, after George had left him. ('I held myself responsible for George's tenets as well as my own,' he explained, 'and wished to set him a good example, he being well-disposed, and given to my guidance, with no harm as yet in any of his ways.')

Throughout the long journey of 1846 George went cheerfully about his duties, recording it all. 'Up at 4, 4.30 or 5, depart at 5, 5.30 or 6, as the case may be, he wrote—much more frequently than the nine o'clock Ruskin remembered later,—though seven or eight o'clock seems to have been the normal departure time. 'To-day, day of rejoicing, finished my writing for Master', recorded George, after five days of writing while at St Martin, near Chamonix. He held the umbrella while 'Master' drew, accompanied him on climbing expeditions while the older people stayed in the valley—and everywhere carried the daguerreotype box which Ruskin called 'little' but which George found cumbersome, although he loved making his experiments with the new instrument, particularly when they were successful.

JOHN

In 1846 Ruskin had published the second volume of *Modern Painters* and by 1848 he was enjoying some literary fame. He was twenty-nine years old and work to him was his whole life. He was suffering from exhaustion following the intense work involved in completing the two volumes and, characteristically, the only effective form of restoration he could find was even more concentrated work, but on a different subject. He therefore decided to turn away from painting in favour of architecture and for this it would be necessary to study the Gothic cathedrals of northern France. It was to be ten years before he would return to, and finish, *Modern Painters*.

Two things delayed Ruskin's departure for the Continent. 1848 was the year of Revolution throughout Europe and from England it was hard to judge what damage the mobs were capable of causing in France. Secondly, it was only four months since his marriage to Effie, a pretty Scottish girl of nineteen whose name was really Euphemia Chalmers Gray; it was a little soon to subject her to the rigours of one of his fact-finding tours. He tried to make do with what was available in the way of Gothic architecture at home and took her to Salisbury; his father and mother went too. When his projected book was ultimately published as *The Seven Lamps of Architecture* he wrote in the preface: 'I have always found it impossible to work in the cold interiors of our cathedrals' and added that the consequence of the few days' work in Salisbury 'was a state of weakened health, which I may be permitted to name among the causes of the slightness and imperfection of the present Essay.'

There was another reason for Ruskin's anxiety to get away as soon as possible from the cold of the English cathedrals to those of France. If the French cathedrals had escaped destruction by the mob they were, he feared, exposed to an even worse hazard—destruction by the restorer. Restoration, to Ruskin, was equivalent to destruction and, if he was to see the churches in their original condition, there was no time to be lost. When later, in the preface to the *Seven Lamps*, he apologised for the delay in publishing the third volume of *Modern Painters,* Ruskin offered as his excuse that his 'whole time has lately been occupied in taking drawings from one side of buildings of which masons were knocking down the other'. Although he already knew the cathedrals of Abbeville, Rouen and Beauvais intimately, the first two must be seen again, as well as the cathedrals of Normandy which, apart from Rouen, he did not know. He believed 'the French nation was, in the twelfth and thirteenth centuries, the greatest in the world; and that the French not only invented Gothic architecture, but carried it to a perfection which no other nation has approached, then or since'.

By August the Second Republic seemed to have settled down in France and the revolutionary spirit had cooled everywhere except in Persia. This was far enough away for safety and Ruskin begged permission to start on his travels.

His parents not only agreed but Mr Ruskin decided to go with them as far as Boulogne. He could not allow himself to be left out altogether.

MURRAY

'Murray did not then exist,' wrote Ruskin of his earlier tours abroad but by 1848 Murray fortunately did exist. When John Murray III had first visited the Continent as a young man the thing he had found most wanting was a good English guide-book and he resolved to write one himself. The result was *Murray's Hand-book for Travellers in Holland, Belgium and North Germany* which was published in 1836 and so warmly was the idea welcomed that by 1848 he was advertising more than sixty 'Works for Travellers'.* They included Hand-books for all European countries (among them Richard Ford's still famous one for Spain) and others dealing with Travel Talk, Painting, The Sanative Influence of Climate and The Domestic Manners of the Russians. Outside Europe the Hand-books covered Egypt, Greece and Turkey as well as Mexico and the Rivers Amazon and Andes. The Englishman's longing to explore beyond his island was quickening and Murray recognised his need for information to ease the problems of getting to his destination and enhance his enjoyment once there.

Murray always turned to the leading authority for the benefit of his readers and he had commissioned Ruskin to contribute articles on Italian painting to the 1847 edition of the *Hand-book*

* Baedeker (who published Handbooks, not Hand-books) had started even earlier with *Die Rheinreise* in 1828 but he left the English field entirely to Murray until he published his first English edition in 1861.

NOTICE TO THIS EDITION.

THE Editor of the 'Hand-book for Travellers in France' requests that travellers who may, in the use of the Work, detect any faults or omissions which they can correct *from personal knowledge*, will have the kindness to mark them down on the spot and communicate to him a notice of the same, favouring him at the same time with their names—addressed to the care of Mr. Murray, Albemarle Street. They may be reminded that by such communications they are not merely furnishing the means of improving the Hand-book, but are contributing to the benefit, information, and comfort of future travellers in general.

*** No attention can be paid to letters from innkeepers in praise of their own houses; and the postage of them is so onerous that they cannot be received.

CAUTION TO TRAVELLERS.—By a recent Act of Parliament the introduction into England of *foreign pirated Editions* of the works of British authors, in which the copyright subsists, *is totally prohibited*. Travellers will therefore bear in mind that even a single copy is contraband, and is liable to seizure at the English Custom-house.

CAUTION TO INNKEEPERS AND OTHERS.—The Editor of the Hand-books has learned from various quarters that a person or persons have of late been extorting money from innkeepers, tradespeople, artists, and others, on the Continent, under pretext of procuring recommendations and favourable notices of them and their establishments in the Hand-books for Travellers. The Editor, therefore, thinks proper to warn all whom it may concern, that recommendations in the Hand-books are not to be obtained by purchase, and that the persons alluded to are not only unauthorised by him, but are totally unknown to him. All those, therefore, who put confidence in such promises may rest assured that they will be defrauded of their money without attaining their object. English travellers are requested to explain this to Innkeepers in remote situations, who are liable to become victims to such impositions. Notices to this effect have been inserted by the Editor in the principal English and Foreign newspapers.—1847.

Notice and title page of Murray's
Hand-book for Travellers in France, 1848

HAND-BOOK

FOR

TRAVELLERS IN FRANCE:

BEING

A GUIDE

TO

NORMANDY, BRITTANY;

THE RIVERS LOIRE, SEINE, RHÔNE, AND GARONNE;

THE FRENCH ALPS, DAUPHINÉ, PROVENCE,

AND THE PYRENEES:

WITH

DESCRIPTIONS OF THE PRINCIPAL ROUTES, *RAILWAYS*, THE APPROACHES
TO ITALY, THE CHIEF WATERING PLACES, ETC.

WITH FIVE TRAVELLING MAPS.

Third Edition, Revised.

LONDON:

JOHN MURRAY, ALBEMARLE STREET.

A. & W. GALIGNANI & CO., STASSIN & XAVIER, PARIS;
LONGMAN, LEIPZIG.

———

1848.

*for Northern Italy.** In later years Ruskin complained ̄that Murray encouraged the traveller to see too much, rather than only what he 'could understand and remember'. In 1848, though, he approved of Murray.

He could hardly do otherwise for the Hand-book was a cornucopia of invaluable information. Having started with simple tables explaining the monetary system (the Bank of France did issue notes but for no sum under 500 francs and they were best avoided as they were difficult to change) and the decimal system of weights and measures, it went to the heart of the matter and gave instruction on the need for, and method of acquiring, a passport.

Readers of *A Sentimental Journey* will remember that Laurence Sterne had been in France for several weeks before he discovered that he had forgotten to take a passport with him. Not that this would have mattered except that France and England were at war at the time and although the war did not prevent the English travelling it did oblige them to carry a passport if they chose to do so. Sterne merely went to the Count de B**** who made one out for him; but a hundred years later, far from being liberalised, formalities had become more difficult,† even though England and France were no longer at war.

You could get your passport free of charge from the French Passport Office in London or, for £2:7:0, from the British

* Ruskin's reputation as an authority was based entirely on *Modern Painters,* which Murray had refused even to read when Ruskin's father had submitted the first volume to him. 'The public care nothing for Turner,' said Murray, ignoring the fact that it was to *make* the public care for Turner that Ruskin had written the book.

† As an example of Murray's prodigious efforts to keep his Hand-books up to date, it may be noted that the 1848 Hand-book for France was not a new edition, nor did it even claim to be a revision of the 1847 edition. Yet a whole page had been reset to take a footnote on the relaxed strictness regarding passports since the introduction of the railroads in France. Other pages were reset to take in a couple of lines about a timber-yard in Calais where Lady Hamilton's remains were interred and others for a warning that 'the high road to Paris is nearly deserted by travellers now that the railway is open to Paris'. John Murray III was himself the Editor and, in his own words, he had 'covered the ground with a network of routes described from personal observation'.

Foreign Office, and Murray saw no virtue at all in the latter: 'it is liable to be taken away at the French frontier like any other'. In its place you would be issued with a *passe provisoire* but the getting of this was a tedious business owing to the number of applicants all eager to start by diligences, railroads or river steam-boats after landing at a French sea-port. The passport itself was then posted to Paris and the traveller had no alternative but to wait there until it arrived and received the signature of the Minister of the Interior. If you were not going to Paris and not leaving France, the original passport *could* be sent to another large town but, warned Murray, if there is a danger of delay in transmitting it to the capital, there is greater in sending it to a provincial place. And you never knew when you might need it. The gendarmes, insisted Murray, 'may stop you on the highway, or waylay you as you descend from the diligence—may force themselves into the *salle à manger* or enter your bedroom to demand a sight of this precious document. It is needless to expatiate on this restraint,' he ended, 'so inconsistent with the freedom an Englishman enjoys at home, or to show that the police are a pest to the harmless and well conducted without being a terror to evil doers; it is the custom of the country, and the stranger must conform or has no business in it.'

The need for his readers to conform to the custom of the country was a favourite theme of Murray's. The unpopularity of the English on the Continent disturbed him profoundly. In the first place, he reflected, 'it arises from the number of ill-conditioned persons (*mauvais sujets*) who, not being in condition to face the world at home, scatter themselves over foreign lands and bring no little discredit upon their country. But there are also many respectable and wealthy persons who, through inattention, wanton expenditure in some cases, niggardly parsimony in others, in general an unwillingness to accommodate themselves to the feelings of the people they are among, bring their own nation into disrepute.' He allowed that we were not always as bad as we seemed to foreigners. The morose sullenness attributed by them to the Englishman was, in his opinion, in nine cases out of ten, nothing more than involuntary silence arising from his ignorance of foreign languages.

This catalogue of the Englishman's imperfections ended strangely in view of the type of reader intended to benefit from the Hand-book. Our countrymen, it appeared, 'have a reputation for pugnacity in France: let them therefore be especially cautious not to make use of their fists, however great the provocation, otherwise they will rue it. No French magistrate or judge will listen to any plea of provocation; fine and imprisonment are the offender's inevitable portion.'

With these words ringing in their ears, perhaps, Mr Ruskin, John and Effie, together with George, set off from Denmark Hill for Folkestone on Monday, August 7, 1848. All were well equipped with pens and paper although George did not keep a day-to-day diary as he had in 1846 (and was to again in 1849). Instead, he filled the gap as well as he could later from memory in ten pages of notes beginning: 'Left London for a short tour of Normandy of which I kept no journal, for which I am now vexed; it was to make up a little for the disappointment of not having the proposed marriage tour, occasioned by the breaking out of the French Revolution in February of this year and subsequently in June'.

THE CROSSING

The railway had just opened from Boulogne to Abbeville, making it possible for the first time to travel from London to Paris entirely by rail and sea (the Abbeville–Paris line had been open for some time; there was as yet no line from Calais). The Ruskins therefore decided to cross the channel via Folkestone and Boulogne instead of via Dover and Calais as had been their custom in the past. John and his father must many times have passed through Boulogne, but to stay there was a new experience.

The Crossing

A steamer went from Folkestone at every tide and ten trains a day from London to Folkestone, so there was every reason for the break with precedent and it may well have been that the novelty of the journey and a sight of the new railway at Boulogne provided an additional inducement for Mr Ruskin to join in the first stage of the journey.

Effie's first letter home described the crossing: 'We went on board the steamer at three and though it was a lovely day I went downstairs and the Ladies Cabin being full I went into the General Cabin and laid down all my length with a gentleman ditto at each end and so on all round with one or two on the floor. In about ten minutes all the Ladies were ill and when two or three heavy lurches came in the middle of the Channel the whole assembly rose en masse from their reclining position dreadfully sick. I was very ill about eight times and Mr Ruskin coming down once said it was like a scene of the plague or something. The Stewards however were very attentive and brought me some nice eau-de-cologne which revived me a little, but the worst was a German or Frenchman whose moustache, Imperial and beard nearly covered his face, being besides a very large man. He was in a dreadful state and moaned and groaned and roared terribly. However at half past five we landed and were ushered into a custom house where our passports were looked at by some soldiers dressed in green and after that we took a Fly and went to the Hotel des Bains, Boulogne, where John and Mr Ruskin immediately broke into raptures at being again in France and the inferiority of England which amused me very much'. It was the first time Effie had been abroad.

Everyone soon recovered from the crossing and they all spent the evening with an English friend who was staying in Boulogne 'for his health'. He told them that in Paris the previous Thursday there had been nothing to be seen but soldiers. The next morning they watched cannon being unloaded from ships in the harbour and heard that the French had declared war with Austria and 'gone over the Alps'. (There was no truth in this rumour.) Then they went to the newly-opened railroad station and Mr Ruskin, in his own words, saw his 'son and his wife off by rail to Abbeville, where he is in his element among cathedrals and tumble-down houses.'[5] Mr Ruskin himself, knowing what would await him if he went on to Abbeville, then abandoned himself to the delights of another steamer crossing back to Folkestone.

ABBEVILLE

John was indeed in his element. 'I was dancing round the table this forenoon,' he wrote to his father the following day, 'in rapture with the porch here—far beyond all my memories or anticipation—perfectly superb, and all the houses more fantastic, more exquisite than ever; alas! not all, for there is not a street without fatal marks of restoration, and in twenty years it is plain that not a vestige of Abbeville, or indeed of any old French town will be left . . . I got into a café and have been doing my best to draw the Cathedral porch; but alas, it is not so easily done. I seem born to conceive what I cannot execute, recommend what I cannot obtain, and mourn over what I cannot save.'

'John is out sketching St Wolfram from a café opposite,' confirmed Effie to her mother. 'As it is so wet and has been raining for ten days we came here to the Hotel de l'Europe which is a splendid place in a large court with nobody in it but ourselves. Mr Ruskin left us at Boulogne to go home; the railway was delightfully comfortable and the carriages much more comfortable and better fitted up than any I have seen in England and better as to punctuality but no passengers scarcely; the poor people here say the revolution has ruined them and they wanted nobody but Louis Philippe and it is only these villains in Paris who have caused all the misfortunes.'

Ruskin's sketches of St Wolfram were made in one of the

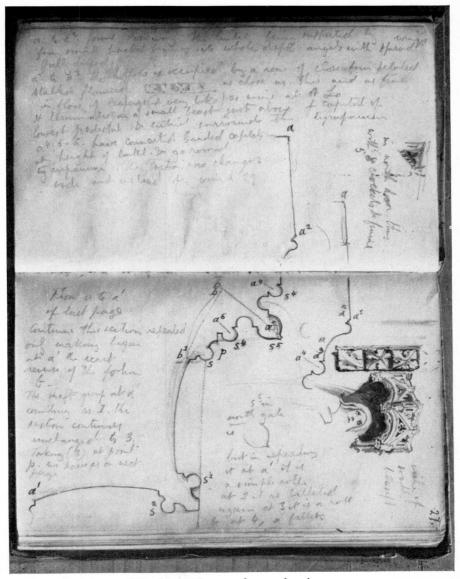

1. Pages from one of Ruskin's Normandy notebooks

2. A French diligence of the 1840s

3. The Market Place, Abbeville, by John Ruskin

4. Entrance to the south transept, Rouen Cathedral, by John Ruskin

eight notebooks, all packed with written and drawn records for his book on architecture, with which he returned home.* In a way it is surprising that he took so much trouble over what was purely documentation when he could have saved time by using the daguerreotype. He knew it well and had described it in the first volume of *Modern Painters*. In 1845 he had written to his father that 'Daguerreotypes taken by this vivid sunlight are glorious things. It is nearly the same thing as carrying off the palace itself'—but that was from Venice and it may have been the lack of vivid sunlight that deterred him now. It is possibly significant that Murray's *Hand-book for Italy* of 1846 contained an advertisement for a Portable Photographic Apparatus for five guineas from John Lee of 440 West Strand whereas no such advertisement appeared in the hand-book for France.

As for the train, it was reasonable that it should be better fitted than those Effie knew in England for it was much newer. The newly opened line reduced the time for the journey from Boulogne to Paris (170 miles) to nine hours against the fourteen hours taken by the diligence. 'The carriages', wrote Ruskin, 'are as large as Great Western and better padded but not slow.'

Murray's opinion of the Abbeville houses was closer to Mr Ruskin's than John's. 'Those who will penetrate into its narrow and filthy streets will find some quaint specimens of ancient domestic architecture, timber houses, etc. but the chief object of interest is St Wolfram.'

It was certainly Ruskin's chief object of interest in 1848 as it had been before and would be throughout his life. 'I have wasted years in mere enjoyment of the Alps', he wrote fifty years later, 'but I never, to my knowledge, wasted an hour in Abbeville or Rouen.' 'For cheerful, unalloyed unwearying pleasure, the getting in sight of Abbeville on a fine summer afternoon,

---

* Plate 1 shows a page from one of them, now at Bembridge. Ruskin's drawing, Plate 3, showing St. Wolfram in the background, was made from near the Hotel de l'Europe in 1868.

jumping out of the courtyard of the Hotel de l'Europe, and rushing down the street to see St Wulfran again before the sun was off the towers, are things to cherish the past for,—to the end.'

DINNER

'I was quite delighted with the cooking, so many little nice dishes and so neat,' ended Effie's letter home. 'Yesterday, although nobody had been here for some time and we only gave them one hour's notice, we had beautiful soup, eels and fried potatoes, mutton chops, stewed woodcock and delicious roasted snipes, with young peas, gruyère cheese, and Vanilla cream, and for desert fresh Filberts, Pears, apricots, Plums, currants, and little cakes, but all so neat and in such little dishes that it did not appear a large dinner. The rooms are beautiful and there is a fine garden with quantities of Balsams and carnations. We remain here till Monday and if you direct my letters to Denmarkhill* I will get them perhaps safer and it will save you the postage. You would really be quite delighted to see how happy John is in a place he likes, and the raptures he is in quite amuse me.' But Ruskin assured his father that he had taken no potatoes and, as for petits pois, 'only what would lie on a point'.

The meal that 'did not appear a large dinner' was Effie's first in France proper, for Boulogne hardly counted as France. It had become, according to Murray, 'since the peace, one of the chief British colonies abroad; and, by a singular reciprocity, on the very spot where Napoleon proposed the invasion of our shores, his intended victims have quietly taken possession and settled themselves down. The town is enriched by English money; warmed, lighted and smoked by English coal; English signs and advertisements decorate every other shop door, inn, tavern and lodging-house; and almost every third person you meet is either a countryman or speaking our language.'

* Mr Ruskin's large house in Camberwell.

Abbeville

There was nothing like this about Abbeville which, moreover, boasted two hotels Murray marked 'very good', a rare tribute from him. The Hotel de l'Europe fell into the first of the two classes he described: 'they are met with along the great roads to Paris, and thence to the South, and make some pretension to study English tastes and habits (and a few of them have some claim to be considered comfortable)—but, being frequented by Englishmen, are very exorbitant in their charges.'

Yet the Hotel de l'Europe charged only three francs (less than half-a-crown) for its table d'hôte which Murray regarded as the 'usual charge'. In remote places and small inns, he warned, 'never order dinner at a higher price than this: the people have only the same food to present even if they charge 10 francs'. In a hotel such as the Europe, though, dinner would have been ordered 'in private'—respectable townspeople, or ladies, would rarely resort to the table d'hôte. Murray well knew the sort of people the table d'hôte company consisted of—'*commis voyageurs,* Anglicé bagmen, but of a stamp very inferior to those of the same class in England'. It was, he said, 'impossible to have sojourned in France for any length of time without the conviction that a more selfish, depraved and vulgar, if not brutal, set does not exist, and gentlemen will take good care not to encourage their approaches, and to keep at a distance from them. They commonly sit down to table with their hats on, scramble for the dishes, so that the stranger who is not on the alert is likely to fare very ill; and if females be present, not only do they not pay them that attention which is customary in all civilised countries at a dinner-table, and used at one time especially to distinguish the French, but, as Mrs Trollope remarks, constantly "use language which no Englishman would dream of uttering in their presence", evincing an utter want of all sense of decency and propriety.'

If this was fair comment it was, perhaps, fortunate for Effie's first impressions of France that the hotel was empty.

The other class of hotel which Murray described consisted

of 'those in remote situations, not yet corrupted to exhorbitance by the English and their couriers, where the traveller who can conform with the customs of the country is treated fairly and charged no higher than a Frenchman'.

Summing up the inns of France, he found them very inferior to those of Germany and Switzerland, in want of general comfort, and above all of cleanliness—their greatest drawback. There is an exception to this, he said, in the bed and table linen. 'Even the filthy cabaret, whose kitchen and salon are scarcely endurable to look at, commonly affords napkins and table-cloths, clean, though coarse and rough, and beds with unsullied sheets and white draperies, together with well-stuffed mattresses and pillows, which put German cribs to shame. Many of the most *important essentials* [Murray's italics], on the other hand, are utterly disregarded, and evince a state of grossness and barbarism hardly to be expected in a civilised country; the provisions for personal ablution are very defective; the washing of floors, whether of timber or tile, seems unknown. In the better hotels, indeed, the floors are polished as tables are in England, with brushes attached to feet instead of hands; but in most cases they are black with the accumulated filth of years, a little water being sprinkled on them from time to time to lay the dust and increase the dark crust of dirt.'

In one respect, however, Murray found the inns of France more accommodating than those of Germany—'they will furnish at almost any hour of the day, at 10 minutes or ¼ hour's notice, a well dressed dinner of 8 or 10 dishes, at a cost not greatly exceeding that of the table d'hôte. The traveller should specify the price at which he chooses to be served, fixing the sum at 3, 5 or more francs, as he may please'—remembering always the previous warning that in remote places the people have only the same food to present, whatever the price.

The Ruskins stayed in Abbeville for a week. Every morning they were up at six and John drew, measured and made notes while Effie wrote up the previous day's notes, and George helped in the research by tracing bas-reliefs. At half past one they dined and 'then', John wrote to his father, 'I am at Effie's service till four, then I draw again till six and come in again to a cutlet and a sip of tea—to bed at nine and up at six so as to get in a little reading before breakfast.'

When not writing up John's notes, Effie conscientiously read French; she found Dumas the best for learning modern French although she did not think as much of him as of Balzac. She enjoyed the walk in the country which they took every afternoon (while John was at her service) and went to her first Catholic Mass at St Vulfran (as it is now spelt) where she was 'confounded with the mixture of the grand and ridiculous in the whole scene'. 'There were but six men among the whole congregation as it was the custom for them to sit at their shop doors smoking long pipes, all the shops being open and the families sitting round the doors with groups among them of the 4th Cavalry with their helmets and long plumes. Everyone seemed so *happy*', and she went on to describe a little child in a white muslin frock and black velvet spencer who was dancing on high stilts to a man playing a trumpet while a mounted band rode past. 'You may imagine my astonishment accustomed to the quiet of a Scotch Sabbath.'

'Effie says France agrees with her perfectly,' John wrote to his father, 'and she certainly seems to enjoy the clear air as much as you or I. She chats away with the people and is getting on fast with her French.' George noticed this, too, and recorded that they had stopped about a week at Abbeville, 'Mr R. being very busy sketching the Cathedral and other buildings, Mrs R. enjoying vastly the difference, so new to her, of the manners and customs here.'

The political situation was improving and Ruskin commented, 'I trust that the negotiations which France and England have together undertaken will pacify all and that we may have another look at Venice yet before the Doge's palace is bombarded.' A new family had arrived at the hotel and 'the people

look quite cheerful and think old times have come again'. There
was a small cloud in that Mr Ruskin had written to say he was
ill but, against this, Ruskin himself was every day recovering
from the rigours of Salisbury and had risen that morning
'without coughing once—for the first time—for though as I
said the cough has been quite gone the little roughness in the
morning remained'.

EU

They planned to leave Abbeville on Tuesday, August 15,
and cover the seventy-five mile journey to Rouen in three stages.
'As the diligences start at an inconvenient hour—$\frac{1}{4}$ before six—,'
Ruskin ended his last letter from Abbeville, 'and I don't wish
to try Effie too much, I have got a *voiturier* to Dieppe.' They were
to sleep at Eu, twenty-one miles from Abbeville, on the way,
'then get early into Dieppe [another nineteen miles] in time to
take the railroad for Rouen on Wednesday'. As he finished his
letter a tremendous thunderstorm broke out, and the next day he
wrote, 'I have seldom heard closer rattle upon flash. The poor old
lady here and the daughter ran into the cellar and there remained
until it was all over. The waiter (George said) "began crossing
himself like anything" and the lady's maid of the English family
here ran away into her room to pull the steel out of her stays.'
Apart from the early starting hour of the diligence to Eu, the
extravagance of the private *voiture* was justified as from Eu to
Dieppe there was not even a diligence, only what Murray
described as a 'rudely jolting, one-horse *patache*'. He warned the
traveller not to expect too much, even from a privately hired
voiture which was likely to be a cabriolet—'a heavy, lumbering
and *jolting* vehicle. . . . It has neither the neatness nor the lightness
of the gigs furnished at a country inn in England but is neces-
sarily clumsily built to stand the terrible cross roads of France.'
Anything, though, was better than the *patache*—'a rustic cab,

verging towards the covered cart, without its easy motion. He who rides in a *patache* must prepare to be jolted to pieces.' Ruskin had evidently read his Murray carefully before deciding not to 'try Effie too much'.

In the event, although Ruskin wrote that the journey from Eu had been 'somewhat tiresome', they had a 'nice coach with plump cushiony red cotton velvet all over it going at the pace of some 4 miles an hour from Abbeville'. They set off at eleven, reached Eu at two and there they dined 'hardly able to hear ourselves speak owing to the celebration of the Fête of the Assumption. There was a fair in honour of the Virgin—much selling of rosaries—two parties of jugglers—beating of drums *à l'envie l'un de l'autre*—blowing of trumpets and roaring to purpleness of face—but the best of it all was a quack doctor in an old cabriolet . . . Effie laughed and was shocked alternately and could neither laugh nor be conscientious with comfort . . . then we went and saw the Chateau—and all the new pictures of our Queen's visit there—and Effie was immensely pleased with all the portraits—the one that interested *me* the most was a "Maximilien de Béthune, duc de Sully" as like *our* Maximilien de Béthune* as it is possible for a face with a long beard to be to a face with a short one. The Chateau is still well kept and cared for and the people are of course *now* very sorry they have lost their King.'

Louis-Philippe had received Queen Victoria at the chateau of Eu a few years before his fall and had fitted up the chateau lavishly for the visit as well as filling it with pictures from top to bottom. Effie was not really 'immensely pleased' with them. She wrote to her mother that she found the whole place 'very melancholy—all the Condés, Montmorencies and D'Artois I should think in French history, and none, either ladies or gentlemen, remarkable for beauty. The room is fitted up with Pictures of the Queen's visit but the Ladies' dresses look

---

* A descendant of the duc de Sully, Henri IV's chief Minister, he had married Caroline Domecq, one of the daughters of Mr Ruskin's partner, Peter Domecq.

shockingly vulgar although only four or six years ago. The Hotel was very disagreeable and redolent of French smells in every variety.' Murray's judgment was confirmed; there were two inns, according to him, 'neither good nor cheap', and Eu, in his opinion, was a 'rather lifeless town' unless, as in the Ruskins' case, you were there on Assumption Day. Effie, too, reported on the quack doctor 'with a man behind beating a drum for effect exhorting all the people to try his oil to cure all diseases; the energy he displayed was perfectly wonderful and we saw him for four hours never cease and he had been there all day'.

George remembered Eu vividly, even after their return. 'The Palace wasn't so much injured as I expected to see it,' he noted, 'the rooms are very grand, an immense number of portraits and pictures hanging on the walls, some of them very interesting indeed, all the old warriors and members of the Orleans family, that were living centuries ago, and not only French but English. I saw the gallery full of paintings by English and French artists of Louis Philippe's and our Queen's visit to each other, some of them very good to my mind. The tapestry seemed a little faded, no doubt when new it was very gorgeous.'

DIEPPE

The next morning the Ruskins continued in their hired *voiture* to Dieppe but they merely passed through the town to join the newly opened railroad for the thirty-five miles from Dieppe to Rouen. Neither seemed to be aware of the chequered history of the Dieppe-Rouen line.

A straight line between London and Paris passes through Dieppe so that, although the Brighton–Dieppe sea crossing used to take eight hours against the two hours of the Folkestone–Boulogne or Dover-Calais crossings, the total distance from London to Paris was far shorter via Dieppe than by the other routes. The fifteen-hour diligence journey from Dieppe to Paris was reduced by four-and-a-half hours when the Rouen–Paris railroad was opened in 1843 but the uncomfortable diligence drive of thirty-five miles from Dieppe to Rouen still took six hours. Ever since the 1830s, when the first project had been initiated, it had been recognised that a railroad to Rouen would make all the difference to Dieppe's prosperity. When it became known that a traveller would be able to cover the 119 miles between Abbeville and Paris in six hours the need became even clearer if Dieppe was to maintain its competitive position.

There was opposition, of course. Soldiers, it was said, would become effeminate if marching were replaced by comfortable railway travel. Train journeys would cause colds, catarrh and congestion of the lungs. Then there was a terrible accident at Versailles when fifty people were killed and the project was abandoned. There was a second attempt to raise the money but this, too, failed. At last, in 1845, an agreement was signed between French and English bankers and provided the occasion 'for the greatest rejoicings Dieppe had ever seen. Cannons thundered from the castle and steeples pealed with bells all day. At night there were balls and revels and at dawn the choral society crept under the windows of the principal signatories to sing them *aubades* composed for the occasion.' No railroad was started, though. In 1847 work really did begin and in 1848 it stopped. The revolution had broken out and Louis-Philippe and his Queen were smuggled out of the neighbouring port of Le Havre and borne to the safety of Claremont in England.

As soon as the new Republic was founded the French went back to work on the railway which had been begun by the English and abandoned by them when they left France at the outset of the Revolution. There was not a great deal to be done and, on July 29, 1848, the great ceremony of inaugurating Dieppe's long-hoped-for railway took place. It had been largely an English undertaking from beginning to end, as had the Rouen–Paris line, and the English engineers and workmen had

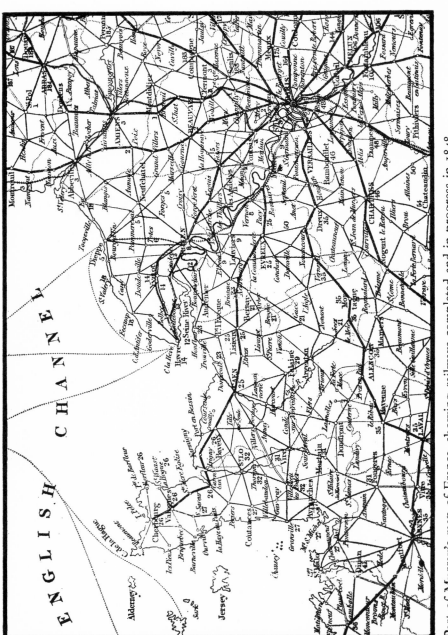

Part of Murray's map of France, showing railways completed and in progress in 1848

been invited to take part in the opening of the railway they had begun. The English had financed it, designed it and for the most part built it, and, perhaps to demonstrate the Englishness of the railway system, the trains ran on the left side ignoring the fact that they were 'abroad'.[7]

Less than three weeks later John and Effie Ruskin drove straight through the town of Dieppe, entered the new station and embarked on the train, apparently taking it all as a matter of course. Effie admired the country of wooded hills and vales. ('I had no conception France was so lovely,' she wrote, 'we have nothing in Scotland or England like the multitudes of trees planted as they are here'.) Murray, the seasoned traveller, on the other hand, found the valleys pleasing but the high table-land monotonous. Indeed, 'during the whole ride there is not one object to excite curiosity'.

At Malaunay the railway joined the Rouen–Havre line and soon a pretty view appeared of the blue hills which bordered the Seine. An envelope of smoke hovered—as over all great manufacturing centres—but it was not as bad as some because here they used good English coal. They were at Rouen.

ROUEN

Rouen at the time was the fifth city of France, with 92,000 inhabitants, three-quarters of the present population. To Murray it had 'the advantage over most other ancient towns that it was not a mere heap of dry bones, destitute of life and abandoned by commerce. Its narrow streets of gable-faced, timber-fronted mansions, swarm like an anthill with busy crowds passing to and fro; it is a focus of trade, and the chief seat of the cotton manufacture in France'. Carried away with enthusiasm he ended: 'It may be called, indeed, the French Manchester.'

Ruskin saw it differently. It was his fifth visit to the city and many years later, in *Praeterita*, he was to write, 'I must here, in advance, tell the general reader that there have been, in sum, three centres of my life's thought: Rouen, Geneva and Pisa. All that I did at Venice was bye-work . . . but Rouen, Geneva, and Pisa have been tutresses of all I know and were mistresses of all I did, from the first moments I entered their gates.' (Geneva, the inclusion of which may puzzle the reader, meant Chamonix as Ruskin later explained.) To him Rouen was a 'labyrinth of delight, its grey and fretted towers, misty in their magnificence of height, letting the sky like blue enamel through the foiled spaces of their crowns of open work; the walls and gates of its countless churches wardered by saintly groups of solemn statuary, clasped about by wandering stems of sculptured leafage, and crowned by fretted niche and fairy pediment— meshed like gossamer with inextricable tracery . . . lightened only here and there by a sunbeam glancing down from scaly backs, and points, and pyramids of Norman roofs, or carried out of its narrow range by the gay progress of some snowy cap or scarlet camisole.'[8] [Plate 5.]

Effie's feelings were somewhere between Murray's and her husband's. 'We are in the Hotel D'Albion very comfortable and a nice Piano. The Cathedral here is perfectly marvellous and the beautiful flower market with women like this [sketch by Ruskin] immediately under the superb edifice. John is perfectly frantic with the spirit of restoration here, and at other places the men actually before our eyes knocking down the time worn black with age pinacles and sticking up in their place new stone ones to be carved at some future time; you could not conceive they could be such idiots and worse if you did not see it.* John has just sketched in this cap in pencil and I have just

* Ruskin's observations on restoration were no more consistent than on most other subjects—was he not to say, 'I am never satisfied that I have handled a subject properly until I have contradicted myself at least three times'? (*Works*, 5, p. liv.) He later modified the view expressed above by writing, 'The single principle is, that after any operation whatsoever necessary for the safety of the building, every external stone should be set back in its actual place: if any are added to strengthen the walls, the new stones, instead of being made to resemble the old

put in the ink and marked where the lace is and the cords in the Muslin which is a single piece much starched and waves back and forwards with the wind. John is going to have some Daguerrotypes taken of the Churches as long as they are standing. It is valuable as they are destroying them so fast. . . . He says he is quite happy in seeing I enjoy myself so much and if it was not for my gentle mediation he would certainly do something desperate and get put in prison for knocking some of the workmen off the scaffolding, but that I always keep him in good humour and he does not know what he should do without me.'

But it must have been dull for Effie, and Ruskin was well aware of the fact, for three days later, on August 20, he was writing to his mother, 'Poor Effie would be far better off with Papa and you than with me for I go out on my own account and when I come in, am often too tired or too late to take her out—so that unless she likes to come with me, always to the same place, she sometimes does not go out all day—and I sometimes cannot —for fear of cold, and sometimes will not—for fear of losing time, stop with her to look at the shops, the flowers or the people. But she is very good and enjoys herself when she is out and is content to stop at home. Only you have certainly spoiled me, my dear mother, as far as expectations of walks are concerned— by your excellent walking. I had no idea of the effect of fatigue on women. Effie—if I take her, after she is once tired—half a mile round—is reduced nearly to fainting and comes in with her eyes full of tears. If however I can once get her to any place

ones, should be left blank of sculpture, and every one have the date of its insertion engraved upon it. The future antiquary would then still be able to study the history of architecture on the authentic building; in my own work it now takes me at least half the time I have to study a building, to find out first what pieces of it are genuine.' (*Works,* 24, p. 410.) And in an unpublished letter of 1853 to the Rev. Daniel Moore, incumbent of Camden Chapel, Camberwell, he produced a new idea altogether— '. . . had I my way, I would have faithful copies executed not only of windows—but of *whole cathedrals*—rather than bad new designs—and not merely instead of such designs, but with the deliberate purpose of having duplicates of great works, rather than restorations.' (Letter of November 21, 1853, written from Edinburgh about a proposal that Millais should design the replacement of a window in the Camden Chapel. Pierpont Morgan Library, New York.)

where she can rest—she will wait for me three hours together (and I certainly could not always say as much for you). So I carry my camp seat in my pocket—and when I want to make a note of anything, Effie sits down; *n'importe où*—on not the cleanest place always—and is as quiet as a mouse.'

Both of them kept diaries. Ruskin's are a mass of technical descriptions, measurements and detailed drawings, only a small proportion of which were used in the published version of *The Seven Lamps of Architecture*. Every one of them was necessary, though; Ruskin's conclusions were indeed the result of 'personal observation' as he claimed in the Preface, and personal observation to him meant detail, detail and yet more detail.

Effie continued to sit as quiet as a mouse and Ruskin went on working for a little more than a week in Rouen. It was gruelling work. 'The beasts of workmen have scaffolding everywhere—in all the churches at once—and every view is spoiled and mostly for ever,' he wrote home. He made no sketches—'nothing but architectural memoranda, but these I think of great value. . . . If you happen to see Mr Prout* please give him my love—and say that I have had more pleasure than I can tell him from two of his sketches I took with me—and that after all my detailing (and I have been working for upwards of an hour yesterday and to-day upon two *crockets*) I find I never succeed in getting any generally true impression except when I imitate him. And that I am longing to see his sketches of Abbeville and Eu again (nearly) as much as my unseen Turners.' (Mr Ruskin had bought for John some Turner drawings and he was made to send sketches of them to Rouen indicating 'which parts of the pictures are red and which gray and so on and where the light comes from'. Every letter refers to them. 'Have you measured them? I should like to know the size.' 'Where have you put them?' The sketches, when they were sent, were '. . . delightful. They make not my mouth but my eyes water for the drawings.')

* Samuel Prout (1783–1852) was neighbour and close friend to Ruskin and his father and had himself toured Normandy in 1818. Ruskin admired his work passionately, wrote about it profusely and praised it extravagantly.

The Diligence

Towards the end of their stay in Rouen the weather broke and it reminded John and Effie that there was much to be done on the journey which lay ahead and that it was advisable to be on their way while it was still mild. Ruskin intended, in any case, to return to Rouen where he hoped to make 'one large and careful drawing'. His last letter to his father from Rouen on August 22 was full of reassurances:

'Certainly we have no reason at present to congratulate ourselves on good fortune—or France on good character as to weather—Pouring rain all the morning again—but we have been very happy in the Cathedral, and I have learnt nearly all about it.—We are quite well and have always plenty to do indoors or out—I sit and look at your sketches of my Turners and enjoy them in imagination. I am living very carefully taking no vegetables nor fruit—only a few Alpine strawberries for dessert. They are wonderfully fine here. I do not find my expence much increased by having Effie with me for the Innkeepers used to put on my apartment the price of another dinner. We pay 12 fr here for a large sitting room with piano, bedroom and dressing room and they are very glad to have us: for there is literally nobody else in the house. . . . I will take care of cross roads, though I fancy that such characters as you speak of are more likely to get—or to have got—into town, as here, and Amiens—Brussels—Lyons, etc.'

He hoped to get some lovely subjects at Mont St Michel 'which I have a notion has never been drawn'.

THE DILIGENCE

They were now to have their first experience of the diligence which they would get to know very well on their journey. Murray described the French stage-coach or diligence in some detail to his readers. 'It is', he said, 'a huge, lofty, lumbering machine, something between an English stage and a broad-wheeled waggon. It is composed of three parts or bodies joined together: 1. the front division, called Coupé, shaped like a chariot or post chaise, holding 3 persons quite distinct from the rest of the passengers, so that ladies may resort to it without inconvenience, and, by securing all 3 places to themselves, travel nearly as comfortably as in a private carriage. The fare is more expensive than in the other part of the vehicle.

'Next to it comes the Intérieur, or inside, holding 6 persons and oppressively warm in summer.

'Behind this is attached the Rotonde, the receptacle of dust, dirt, and bad company, the least desirable part of the diligence, and the cheapest except

'The Banquette, or Impériale, an outside seat on the roof of the coupé, tolerably well protected from rain and cold by a hood or head, and leather apron, but somewhat difficult of access until you are accustomed to climb up into it. It affords a comfortable and roomy seat by the side of the conductor, with the advantages of fresh air and the best view of the country from its great elevation, and greater freedom from dust than those enjoy who sit below. It is true you may sometimes meet rough and low-bred companions, for the French do not like to travel outside, and few persons of the better class resort to it, except English, and they for the most part prefer it to all others. It is not suited to females owing to the difficulty of clambering up to it.'

Murray's glowing account of the joys of travel in the coupé tempted Ruskin to indulge in the extravagance. 'John had taken the Coupée for himself,' wrote Effie on reaching Lisieux; 'we were very comfortable and saw the six grey horses prancing in front of us in very fine style.'

INTO THE NORMANDY COUNTRY

'The country was perfectly beautiful,' Effie continued, 'and like our richest Highland scenery with the rich cultivation of the South at the bottom of the little Hills. We stopped to breakfast on the road at a little house where we had excellent coffee in bowls, roast fowl, boiled greens, cider and fruit of strawberries and pears. . . . It was pouring rain when we reached [Lisieux] at three and as we could do nothing we dined at the very uncomfortable Inn and felt extremely cold. The people did not seem accustomed to strangers and we could get nothing we wanted. There were some interesting old wooden houses and the Churches were fine, at least one was. Here they gave us the cheese of the country and how the people eat it is a marvel to me for it is small, made of cream and kept until it is in the last stage of decay with the most disgusting smell possible.'*

Ruskin, too, found the drive 'delightful—the diligence seems quite *bright* when you are in it and the coupé is just like your chariot and six—and no trouble with postillions—and view everywhere except behind—but it is expensive—at least taking the three places—one of which of course George would have taken if there had not been room for him outside—they would not give the Coupé except all the way to Caen so there is 16½ francs—multiplied by 3, + 3 francs extra for luggage—= 52½ francs, nearly a days posting but it is really pleasant and faster—and I shall only take two coupés and an outside next time—and if we go the whole way it will be reasonable. But you never saw anything yet in France so lovely as this Normandy—just fancy—vallées like rich bits of Italy—tufted with elder—poplar—willow—and spanish chesnut set between round sweeping grouse hills of purple heather. . . . I think Effie makes the heather grow under her feet. But I never saw such a lovely contrast of purple and green—even in Switzerland where we have the Rose—the green is blacker and not so soft. The sweetest bits of all were the soft flat vale of the Abbaye de Bec—and the approach to this place—rich to excess with its wooden houses all so quaint on the hillside as if it had been all built for pigeons. But the Inns—not to say abominably bad—but so raw and blundering—like Blois—

---

* Undoubtedly the *Livarot*, 'whose strong smell', Michelin admits today, 'alarms the uninitiated'.

only with less desire to oblige—and less naiveté or good humour.'

George was no more used to public transport, when travelling abroad, than Ruskin. 'This was my first ride in a diligence' he noted, 'and I paid my footing, for we stopped to breakfast at a little village on the road, where they demanded six francs, 5*s* for a miserable breakfast not worth a couple, but after a good row I got off by paying four francs. I'll remember that place if I should ever go by that road again; I'll go without anything rather than they shall see my money again, the confounded thieves.'

They stayed only one night at Lisieux which is remarkable in view of the work Ruskin did there. He made a detailed draw-ing of the shafts of the door of the cathedral which he described in *The Seven Lamps of Architecture* as 'one of the most quaint and interesting doors in Normandy'.[9] He added that it was 'probably soon to be lost for ever by the continuance of the masonic operations which have already destroyed the northern tower'. Fifty-five years later the editors of his collected works put a footnote to this passage saying 'a prophecy of doom not hitherto fulfilled', and, by a strange coincidence, when in June, 1944, the entire old town of Lisieux was destroyed by fire during the bombardment, the Cathedral itself was left untouched.

Ruskin also examined the Gothic and Renaissance houses for which the town was famous (all of which were destroyed in 1944) and later described the town's 'wooden street in stone style' in a criticism of a drawing by Prout, who had failed to convey the sense of the architecture in a particular drawing. At the end of the day he still had energy enough to write a long letter to his father on their relationship to God which he ended with the somewhat discouraging words: 'If one were to calculate the averageable life at eighty years, with a doubtful evening after that time, and suppose this represented by a day of sixteen hours from six morning till ten night, I am now at *noon*, you at six in the evening—with both of us the day is far spent—I never think my day worth much after twelve o'clock. And yet I fear—

forgive me if I am wrong—that neither of us have chosen our master or begun our work.'

FALAISE

'Next day', wrote Effie on August 27, 'we left in the diligence for this place [Falaise] at three. The diligences go very slow when they have only two horses and although the distance was only thirty miles we did not reach until nearly nine o'clock, we got to the Hotel de France. The country was most beautiful and the sky heavenly till it got dark. . . . Most of the women and men here wear cotton nightcaps exactly like Papa's with a tassel at the end, the whole of the hair away, and it makes the women look very ugly. High above the Tanneries on a grand rock overhead stands the massive old Castle of Robert Le Diable in which his son William the Conqueror was born; it is a ruin but still very strong. John is making a pretty drawing of it. The people here are very primitive in their habits and for instance the butcher opposite kills everything in the open street and the streams are for a few minutes after running with blood but as the fountains send forth always fresh water it soon disappears; again the people in the houses opposite and alongside empty everything out of the high windows down to catch the said stream which considering the height they throw from they manage very cleverly.'

It was Sunday, August 27, and, as usual when there was no Protestant church, they had been to Mass in the morning after which Ruskin had read the service in their hotel. It was scarcely necessary for them to bear in mind Murray's admonitions to less experienced travellers: 'Englishmen and Protestants, admitted into Roman Catholic churches, at times are often inconsiderate in talking loud, laughing, and stamping with their feet while the service is going on: a moment's reflection should point out to them that they should regard the feelings of those around them who are engaged in their devotions. Above all, they should avoid as much as possible turning their backs upon the altar. In a church ladies and gentlemen should not walk arm in arm—as that is contrary to the usual practice of the people and to their idea of good manners: they should avoid talking together during the service.'

In the evening Ruskin read the service again. The weather was dreadful—'continual rain and wind,' he complained to his father, 'with a variety of thunder and cold—almost frost yesterday morning—so that I could not work out of doors with the least comfort. It loses my time terribly. But this if it were but ordinary weather is the loveliest place conceivable—a valley between granite crags of which I have not seen the end yet—all heather and millstream and exquisite winding walks among orchards and bright meadows and the quaintest architecture in the world. . . . The costumes too are wonderful but the people perfectly barbarous—at least judging from their horrible church service. But they are civil and simple—touch their hats to you in the country and appear good tempered and well conducted on the whole although fearfully lazy. . . . I cannot write you a chat to-day for we have been kept late by a long sermon in the Catholic church and I want to read our own service and the letters must go at two. . . . Effie is so well among the hills that I do not hurry.'

Next day the weather improved and they stayed at Falaise until the following Thursday, a week in all. 'We are enjoying ourselves here exceedingly,' wrote Ruskin, 'I am getting I think a very beautiful view—but I am obliged to stay—for I cannot without overcrowding myself—make a large drawing in much less than a week—and Friday was spent looking about and Saturday was wet. Yesterday was lovely as could be—the most exquisitely French sun and air—and I got on delightfully—worked all the morning sitting in a garden under a great rock with vines trellised all over it—and a walnut tree beside it—and gourds on the ground—and with the great castle and its crags opposite—and then in the afternoon I took Effie up and into the said castle—it is private and kept locked, but they let us in as long as we like—and so we sat on the grass, and walked in the sunny orchard under Talbot's Tower, and peeped about into the niches and passages in the thick walls—and looked out of the window where Robert le Diable looked out and saw the "miller's maiden" down in the valley below—and took her up to his castle and made her his lady—and she was the mother of the Conqueror.* He must have had good eyes for the village street is some 250 feet below—and I have drawn one of the old capitals with a man on it leading a pig—delicious—it is to be hoped antecedent to the 10th century—or it might be hinted that William put it as typical of himself collaring the English swine. And so we rambled about all day nearly—and then took a little walk when it got cooler—and came to an old beggar sitting in a kind of sentry box by the roadside and telling his beads slowly— blind and with a nice rough doggy in the box beside him—a very sad and sweet picture—and an altogether sad reality. We are going to pay him another visit to-day and I shall take him and the doggy some dinner.'

In the evening of the same day, August 29, Ruskin wrote again to his father, 'for I hope to be out all day to-morrow—I have places in the Diligence for Thursday—finding that I must really fix *some* day but I have not half done the place, it is most lovely. I have got a view however which I think you will like. Tell George Richmond† I want—for people always have wants —to have *him* with me to draw all the French ['people' crossed out] bodies in their tall caps and the children and the begger and his dog, and Turner with me to draw the great chateau and the

---

* She is more generally said to have been a tanner's daughter. Ruskin does not mention that before 'making her his lady' Robert asked and obtained her father's permission.

† George Richmond (1809–96) had drawn Ruskin in 1842 and was to make a number of other portraits of him (including one now in the National Portrait Gallery). He became a lifelong friend and influence on Ruskin. He had himself come under Blake's influence and he became a successful portrait painter and R.A.

poplars—and rocks—and Prout with me to draw the churches. I would give them our three places in the coupé if they would come and go on the top.' Frustration was making him testy. 'It is very odd reading your letter here which wondered "whether George passed Falaise without asking". I never pass any place I have once told you to write to. . . . You always write you are "so so"—How do you mean and what is the matter—have you seen Dr Grant?'* Perhaps it was as well that they would soon be on the road again.

Murray described Falaise as 'a dull lifeless town, at present, having only one object of interest to the passing traveller—the *Castle*, one of the few real Norman fortresses remaining in France, and the birthplace of William the Conqueror'.

All that had come out of the Ruskins' week's stay there (except for the drawing which has disappeared) was a one-line reference in the *Seven Lamps* to part of a flying buttress from the apse of St Gervais [Plate 6] with a line drawing of it and another one line reference to the piers of the church in *The Stones of Venice*.

VIRE AND MORTAIN

'Vire is black melancholy—and the Inn the most abominable to my taste that I ever entered—so we set off at seven this morning,' wrote Ruskin. 'At Vire we remained the day, the Inn dirty and uncomfortable, the town so so,' confirmed Effie. 'A miserably dirty hotel as well as town,' was George's comment. 'Not good' was all Murray had to say about the only inn.

The Ruskins had left Falaise at eight in the morning of August 31 and 'our Conductor stopped I should think about a score of times on the road to speak to his acquaintances and first to

* Dr Grant was friend and physician to the Ruskin family. In Effie's first letter home from Abbeville she had written 'at Folkestone we had five minutes chat with Dr Grant and the Miss Sydneys [his step-daughters] who have arrived home after a year's absence' (the girls, probably, not Dr Grant himself).

breakfast and then to dine quite at his ease,' Effie wrote. They were in the open coupé and Effie found 'the country exquisite and the heather fine.'

Vire, according to Murray, was 'a most picturesque antique town, romantically situated on a lofty eminence, bordered by deep ravines'. It had also had the distinction of giving a word to the world, for 'Vaudeville' was originally applied to the merry and humorous drinking songs composed in the two valleys of Vire which were called 'Les Vaux de Vire'.

'The people seemed all very busy and at Vire most of the army clothing is made,' Effie continued knowingly. She had taken the information straight out of Murray who insisted that 'almost all the valleys in the neighbourhood, generally shut in by craggy heights and copse-covered slopes, deserve to be explored. They abound in mills of paper and *cloth*, in which the clothing for the French army is made. This gives employment to half the inhabitants of Vire.'

The Ruskins had just missed the *Fête des drapiers* which, according to Murray, was celebrated on August 10 when 'more than 10,000 persons assemble under the apple trees, which are illuminated at night for the occasion'. Not even Vire's 'gastronomic celebrity for chitterlings (*andouilles*) and pastry' could reconcile them to the place and they set off for Mortain.

Murray found Mortain 'a decayed and lifeless town' but it occupied 'a position nearly resembling that of Vire, and at least equally romantic'. Ruskin could have found little or no work to do there but everything that could be found was dutifully entered in the diary with detailed drawings and, when a plate was drawn for *The Stones of Venice* containing line drawings of twenty-eight 'Profiles of Bases', a base in the nave of Mortain's St Evroult found itself immortalised. It was little enough to show for a stay of five days but it was something.

Murray thought the inn 'improved' and, indeed, 'not bad to stop at', but the Ruskins regretted taking his advice. 'The Inn here is detestable,' wrote Effie, 'we have to pass through a kitchen worse than the one at the Bridge of Tummel to get to our bedrooms. In John's dressingroom we sit and have our meals but the floor of my room is so dirty that if any part of my clothes touch it they are covered with dirt directly and our washing basins are little, so small in fact that every time I wash I send the water over in streams on the table. They have no cups and our breakfast and tea are taken in bowls nearly as large as the basins. The first two days they gave us milk for our coffee out of a large saucepan and the Coffee out of a little tin like what Papa used to have for his shaving water, but George has got us some improvement and I must say the food is excellent.'

'But all this is nothing,' she went on, 'if you saw the exquisite country and John says it is exactly like Tivoli but more beautiful. The rocks, cascades and romantic dells are like the most beautiful scenes of our Killiecrankie and then the immense blue campagnia stretching away for twenty miles, and to the west you just catch the sea with Mont St Michel rising fairly out of it. It is the most splendid thing I ever saw in my life certainly and John says he had no idea there was such beauty here, he never saw anything like it—and the hedges loaded with brambles like bunches of black grapes. There are myriads without exaggeration—every corner you pass are large spreading bushes covered and nobody seems to gather them. We have not seen a single child eating any of them and I cannot help thinking that their laziness even prevents them taking what is just lying to be gathered.'

It was another Sunday and they had been to Mass and found the service 'more sensible than what I have yet seen. . . . We have returned and John, having read the Morning Service, has gone out to walk till dinnertime. I walk with him from four till seven in the evening but the heat just now is too powerful for me—or I should think for anyone but John. He could stand any heat I think and like it for it is like Italy. Mr Ruskin has written us no general news for a long time and we might as well be in Japan for we never see even a French Paper. . . . We go on Tuesday

5. Street in Rouen leading to the south transept of the Cathedral seen in Plate 4. From a photograph in Ruskin's collection

6. St Gervais, Falaise, with old houses joined to it as it was in Ruskin's time

morning [September 5] for a week to Avranches to allow John time for some sketches of St Michel.' At the top of Effie's letter, Ruskin wrote a note: 'I think you would be very happy to see Effie among the heather here—she enjoys the town much but she is enjoyment itself now—so am I in seeing her so.' He was very pleased with Effie for the moment and told his father on this same Sunday: 'Effie and I understand each other perfectly and she accomodates herself to all my ways—only remonstrating when she thinks I draw too much for my health—she is a very good girl.'

Effie had reported Ruskin's enthusiasm for Mortain accurately and at first he could overlook the inn's shortcomings—he rated it 'tolerable'. He found the surrounding country 'so wonderfully like Tivoli that I am obliged to listen for the French accent and look for the Norman caps in order to remember where I am.* It is better than Tivoli in two respects—that the rocks are of granite instead of Tufor—and the campagna instead of a desolate plain is a rolling blue sea of country which *Effie* confesses to be much finer than anything she ever saw in Worcestershire or the best parts of England.—and she is quite right—for such a succession of lovely wooded and pasture land as we have had heaped in hill beyond hill all the way from Lisieux I cannot remember having ever seen in Switzerland.'

The scenery round Mortain captured George as well as the Ruskins. 'From the little hills above the town there was a beautiful view,' he wrote 'on a clear evening of the country round with the plains of Brittany beyond, and at times Mont St Michel was visible, standing out by itself from the sea. I certainly think this is the prettiest part of France that I have seen.'

Mr Ruskin was still being difficult over letters. They were arriving in both England and France with a speed which seems astonishing today (generally Mr Ruskin's note 'answered' bears

---

* Murray quoted 'G. Knight' who had written: 'The whole scene put me in mind of Italy, and of Tivoli, and the cascades which we heard from above and visited afterwards helped to keep up the resemblance.' (*An Architectural Tour in Normandy* by Henry Gally Knight, M.P., John Murray, 1836).

4

a date three days after the date of posting and sometimes only two) but his son was not satisfied that his instructions were being carried out. 'I got a letter of half a sheet before I left Falaise,' he complained, 'with nothing in it, whatever, except advices respecting post offices. Now I cannot manage better than I do—in a country which I am exploring—only whenever I have once said "write to such a place" I mean you to write until I tell you a new one.' George was being sent back to Vire and Falaise to collect the 'scattered epistles' which had resulted from the misunderstandings.

Mr Ruskin was having a difficult time in other respects. His wife was ill and the owner of a house in Park Street which he had taken furnished for his son and daughter-in-law to return to had apparently not fulfilled the agreement to leave certain ornaments and furniture. Ruskin begged his father not to let himself get annoyed about. 'I can get a pitcher or two from the well heads here,' he assured him, 'which are worth all the china which every nymph sighed over cracks in.' 'Don't fight about anything,' he ended, 'there is nothing worth fighting for in houses. If it were to save a niche in a cathedral here from restoration—it could be worth while.'

'Here' must have meant anywhere but in Vire or Mortain for on the next day, September 2, Ruskin, still at Mortain, was writing in a birthday letter to his mother, 'Not that the church *here* is much—for it is built—as well as that of Vire—of native granite and it is impossible to carve granite into Gothic niches.'

'I have made your birthday a day of rest.' he continued, 'and have promised Effie a walk in the rocky valley to make her evening happy. . . . I wish you had been with us—that is whenever I am out of doors—and for my *own* sake when I am indoors too—but certainly not for yours—in fact I am afraid you would not stay at such places—anything more filthy I have not seen—nor more savage in habits—one knife each is as much as we can get for carving—and eating—meat pudding and fruit—milk for coffee brought in a stewpan etc. . . . We are trying to be economical already: Effie likes the diligence travelling very much and I shall not be in the least afraid of going anywhere with her now—and it is a great saving besides the pleasure of having good horses, good drivers and no [indecipherable]. We have all [including George?] drunk your health today at our early dinner—I ordered a bottle of Burgundy therefore for the first time.'

But the next day was clouded for Effie by news from home. Most of her family seemed to be ill, with more illness threatening; and her father's affairs (he had invested disastrously in railway shares) were even worse than they had been before her marriage. 'She was very low all yesterday evening,' Ruskin told his father but he hastened to reassure him: 'She has recovered to-day. Perhaps these matters are all good for us—I am certainly terribly selfish and care little for anything so that I can get quiet—and a good pencil—and a Turner or two—it was and perhaps still is growing upon me—and it may be just as well that I am forced to think and feel a little for others—at least I may think—but I don't feel—even when poor Effie was crying last night I felt it by no means as a husband should—but rather a bore—however I comforted her in a very dutiful way—and it may be as well perhaps on the other hand that I am not easily worked upon by these things.' With this piece of self-analysis Ruskin prepared to leave Mortain early the following morning.

AVRANCHES AND MONT ST MICHEL

'Avranches is considered one of the handsomest towns in Normandy,' wrote Effie on Saturday, September 9, 'but we found it very stupid and uninteresting excepting the beautiful view across the rich plain to the sea and Mont St Michel standing far off; next morning [they had arrived by diligence on the Tuesday] we got an open Cabriolet and started for the Mount—12 miles although looking only about five. The country became as we approached only sand and tamarisk trees and instead of Mont St Michel being in the sea as we expected, it rose hugely and grandly out of the desert of sand the same for many miles round, a dead flat without a single speck on its surface. We drove five miles across and arriving found contrary to all expectation a very nice clean little Inn where we took up our abode. We found that the sea does surround the Mount once a week some feet in depth but owing to the deep flat for so many miles a few feet of tide covers the whole of this desert of sand; you will know the position of it on the map and I have asked John to draw a little sketch of it which I think he has done very well. There is the fine Gothic Church at the top then the Castle holding 500 prisoners and then the little town. . . . We leave on Monday for Coutances and then to Bayeux; we once intended going to Dol and Dinan in Brittany but we think that remaining some time at Caen and Rouen on our way back will bring us not sooner home than the first week of October and I think we should not be longer out of our house than that if we go to Switzerland next year. John and I tried to walk as far as the sea this evening but the sand deceives one so that you walk and walk and seem not a bit farther off the Mount so we gave it up and returning sat down on the rocks and played a game a little like Bowls . . . and now we have come in to have our delicious *Café au lait* which we shall have served as soon as the cows come from the country opposite, where they feed all day, to be milked.'

The mild tone of disappointment over Mont St Michel in Effie's letter came out frankly in Ruskin's. 'I have not often been more disappointed than in this place,' he had written on Friday, September 8, 'and yet on minor grounds—It is not exaggerated by the artists. It is picturesque—beyond bettering, almost—and the interior as a piece of baronial gloom and lordliness, noble above all I ever saw—a sort of Raby castle* grafted on Salzburg. But the drawbacks are quite overpowering. The lovely country which is seen from Mortain stops within some three miles of the

* Near Durham.

Mont St Michel by John Ruskin

coast—and is succeeded by a belt of patchy and ragged cultivation mixed with sand hills which die out into a melancholy flat
of salt sand and tamarisk trees. From this the sands stretch out
as they do at Lancaster—but instead of golden and yellow bright
sand covered twice a day by the sea—they are a *grey* fine sand of
soft clayey granite dust mixed with mud—and having the look
of mud—only singularly enough—these sands are only covered
by the tide about once in six days—and a foot or two deep only:
remaining the rest of the week as we see them now—a waste of
grey dry desert muddy in places—and with a pool or two of
thick salt water but for the most part quite hard—and stretching
so far beyond the Mount that a walk of an hour yesterday did
not bring me to the sea. The weekly tide however is trusted to
by the inhabitants of the mount for ablution of all foulness—and
the consequence is that St Michael's Mount, Normandy—
instead of being like *our* St Michael's—dashed upon by the deep
green sea—and pure and cold in the sea breezes—is surrounded
by a flat of filthy sand, channelled by brown and stinking rivulets
of slow discharge—and spotted by fragments and remnants of
fish and offal and street cleansings. Well—I am prepared to bear
this kind of thing in pursuit of the picturesque but the flat
masses without water are fearful things for wind—and stench. . . .
Now the interior of the castle is in itself magnificent. But
imagine the effect on one's associations and feelings of its being

inhabited by 500 *forçats* [convicts] and the soldiers who guard them. These gentlemen (and French *forçats* look thoroughly what they are) meet you in small files in the corridors, walk for exercise in the *cloisters*—occupy all the chambers as well as the dungeons—and finally *dine* in the transept of the church! while the "Salle des Chevaliers"—certainly the most royal and knightly looking vaulted hall I ever entered—is *entirely* filled from one end to the other with the black and crowded looms at which they work calico. You know it is impossible to make drawings under such depressing circumstances—a certain degree of *feeling* is necessary to success—and it is impossible to feel anything here but Newgate. There is however so much in the architecture that is marvellous that I am going to look at it from the outside for two days more in order that I may not need to undergo the penance of coming here again. I will take care to run no risk of cold or other illness. The mount and castle are said to be perfectly healthy and as the sea is—they say—to come up round us on Saturday or Sunday—I hope to leave on Monday for Coutances with a pleasanter impression of the place. My *voiturier* is ordered and places taken in the diligence coupé for Coutances on Monday—but address now to Bayeux.'

For once neither Effie nor John had read their Murray carefully or they would have known that 'at neap tides the rock is not surrounded by water at all, at any part of the day. At spring tides it is surrounded twice each day, and then the sea sometimes breaks into the soldiers' mess-room.' Murray found Mont St Michel more impressive than did the Ruskins. 'There is something mysterious and almost awful in the aspect of this solitary cone of granite, rising out of the wide, level expanse of sand. One might imagine it the peak of some colossal mountain just piercing through the crust of the earth, but deprived, at the moment of its appearance, of the geological force necessary to rear it aloft. Slight as is its elevation, its isolated position in the midst of the sea, and its heaven-pointed top, render it the prominent view from the surrounding coast, and from a long distance give it the appearance of being much nearer at hand than it really is. On approaching it, it is found to be girt round at its base by a circlet of feudal walls and towers, washed by the sea; above these rise the quaint irregular houses of the little town, plastered as it were against the rock, and piled one over another. Above them project the bare beds of rock, serving as a pedestal from which the lofty walls, high turrets, and prolonged buttresses of the conventual buildings are reared aloft, surmounted in their turn by the pinnacles and tower of the church (now bearing a telegraph) which crowns the whole, and forms the apex of the pyramid.' Such was the scene which Ruskin proposed to spend two days looking at in order not to have to return.

The beautiful little sketch in Effie's letter was all that was ever to come out of Mont St Michel after the high hopes held out in Falaise. Twenty-five years later Ruskin wrote to William Ward*, 'I couldn't draw when I was there, for convicts.' But he could, and did, modest though the drawing is.

The next day, September 9, he wrote that he was still unable to draw; the continual wind and cold draughts made it impossible. Nevertheless, he had 'had a nice rest and recovered lost ground in notes, etc'. He thanked his father for wishing them to stay as long as they liked but added, 'I think I shall not linger much except at Caen and Rouen—The latter is *the* place of north Europe as Venice is of the South. I am a little sorry I left Falaise so soon— I have seen nothing since like it—but I expected too much here.'

Then came a note of anxiety. 'The only thing that we can find to complain of is that Effie loses her hair continually; I wish you would ask my mother or William† or Dr Grant why this is—it is really getting serious—and besides, the thing itself seems to

---

* Ward was originally a pupil of Ruskin's at the Working Men's College and later he became Ruskin's Turner copyist and agent for the sale of Ruskin's photographs as well as an exhibitor at the Royal Academy in his own right. On this occasion (August, 1873) Ruskin had sent Ward off to Mont St Michel and other places in Normandy to do some drawings for him.

† Dr William Richardson, a son of Mr Ruskin's only sister, Jessie.

me a sign of bad health—it comes out in handfuls when it is brushed in the morning—it has come out in the same way ever since she went to Dover' (in the previous June).

For George, Mont St Michel had even unhappier memories. He shared the general disappointment over its situation. 'I had understood this mountain was entirely surrounded by the sea,' he wrote, 'and I had visions constantly floating about me, of sitting on the rocks and fishing, of a nice summer evening, for my supper, so I was very much disappointed when I found that my fishing had turned out a bad speculation, for it was only about once a fortnight or three weeks that the tide ever came up as high as to surround it entirely. . . . On certain days when there would be a good haul of fish of a particular kind, the fishermen would come from miles around, bare legged and carrying each their nets, and on their return there used to be a dreadful noise with them outside the inn where we were stopping. They used to squat on the ground and drink cyder like *thirsty men* and no mistake of it (By the bye, since I left Rouen and until my return, I never had a drop of wine, nothing but cyder in Normandy. I couldn't get on with it at first at all, but gradually became accustomed to it, it is generally very good in Normandy). These men generally drank until the evening and many of them could scarcely keep their legs as they went along.'

To add to the disappointment, there was bad news. 'I was not sorry to leave,' George ended, 'here too I received the news of Tom's intention to be off to Sydney in the November following.' Ruskin reported this to his father in his last letter from Mont St Michel, dated Sunday, September 10: 'George, who is very affectionate, has been quite upset today by hearing that his brother has made up his mind to go to Sydney. It will be some time before he recovers it [sic] but he seems to think his brother is quite right.* Effie is sitting by my side just now writing out

---

* George himself eventually emigrated to Australia where he became a Police Magistrate in New South Wales. He married, had seven children, and died in 1892.

pages from the Proverbs for me—and printing them almost that they may be quite legible and she has written nearly all my diary for me from my dictation—saving my eyes for the present much, though if my eyes are to be saved eventually I am afraid she will have to write it over for me again.'

This is the first mention of Ruskin's eye trouble and it is the last to be heard of it. By the time they reached Coutances, their next stopping place, his eyes had recovered and he was writing his diary himself. How much of it had been written by Effie before will never be known. In the fifth volume of his own series of diaries Ruskin wrote: 'This book begins with 14 pages of Effie's diary . . . beginning at Dover and going on to Abbeville. . . . Then 15 more pages of Effie's diary . . . continuing to January 1849 when I took possession of the book'. Almost forty years later Ruskin must have returned to his diary for the writing of *Praeterita* and have found Effie's handwriting in it unbearable. 'Cut out—1885. J.R.', he wrote against the first reference to her diary and: 'These also cut out 1885. J.R.', he repeated against the second reference. He also tore out, without mentioning it, all the pages of his own diary written before Coutances. There were forty-eight pages of his diary between Abbeville and Caen, according to his own note at the beginning of the book, but there are now only twenty-six left, the first page being numbered twenty-two and headed 'Coutances'.

AVRANCHES AGAIN

At nine in the morning of Monday, September 11, the party of three began their journey back to Rouen on their circular route. They arrived at Avranches in time to catch the diligence and stayed no longer than was necessary. To Effie it was a 'stupid town' and Ruskin did not refer to it at all. According to Murray, though, 'the beauty of the situation, the salubrity of the air, and the cheapness of living' had rendered Avranches a favourite residence of the English who formed a considerable colony there. Apart from Caen and Rouen, which had had English settlers since the eighteenth century, Avranches alone in Normandy claimed this distinction.

The presence of so many fellow countrymen impressed George who wrote: 'There are a great many English emigrants in this neighbourhood who live here entirely, living and other necessaries being so much cheaper; a very tidy house with garden &c, and often prettily situated, may be had I was told for 12 to 20 pounds a year, so that with 80 or 100 pounds a year a family might live with the greatest luxury, plenty of shooting in the country, having to pay a small fee for permission to shoot. It is amusing though, to see the English, endeavouring to be taken for French and not of their own country, mustachios, beards, clothes cut to match as near as possible, but it's no use, any one at all practised can see through them in a moment and when they are found out they talk of their chateaux and forests here, as big and as majestic as they possibly can, but in general they have a broken down, shabby genteel appearance about them, not at all the thing. Still, it's not very surprising that people with a moderate income, which in England would be looked on as barely enough to keep a family at all respectable, should go to a country where with the same amount they could live comfortably and to spare, and be looked upon by the peasantry about them as *milors*, but then they should not be so big and so elevated and give themselves such airs with their new titles.'

Avranches had another claim to fame for it was here, in the eighth century, that Archangel Michael appeared to its Bishop, Aubert. He pointed out to the Bishop that by ancient custom mounts, such as the one then known as Monte Tombe, had had chapels built on their summit dedicated to him, Michael, and that only Bishop Aubert had failed in paying this courtesy. The Bishop was polite but did nothing, and Michael, it is said, appeared again to draw attention to the empty mount. Still nothing was done and a third visit became necessary. This time

Michael was determined to make it clear that his presence was no figment of the Bishop's imagination so he poked his finger into the Bishop's head. Aubert at last woke up to his responsibilities, built the chapel and renamed the mount after St Michael in accordance with usual practice. He was then left in peace during his lifetime but his skull, which can be seen today in St Gervais at Avranches, still shows the mark resulting from temporising with archangels.

Neither was Avranches a 'stupid' town to General Mark Patton. In 1944 it was his headquarters and from it he made the breakthrough that led the American army almost into Germany. Accordingly, Avranches is one of the few towns untouched by the Battle of Normandy, and St Gervais, with the Bishop's head safely preserved, looks out on to the Place Patton.

COUTANCES

'We had rather a hard day's journey from St Michel yesterday,' wrote Ruskin to his father from Coutances on Tuesday, September 12, '—the roads heavy in sand—stopped for an hour or so at Granville—where the sea view is very lovely and put me in mind of Genoa.'

It did not remind Murray of Genoa at all. 'A new town is gradually spreading itself along the low margin of the harbour,' said the Hand-book, 'and up the banks of a stream so small that it is generally swallowed up in soapsuds, and contributes, with the filthy abominations of the town itself, to produce a state of atmosphere barely tolerable. The sombre hues of the buildings, whose walls are dark granite and their roofs black slate, renders Granville on a near examination as unattractive to the sight as to the smell, and moreover it contains no objects of interest.'

There was only one diversion according to Murray for 'the stranger desirous to rescue himself from *ennui*' he could go bathing. But 'there are no machines; instead of them bathers are enclosed in cases of canvas carried in the fashion of sedan chairs, and they must walk into the water thickly clad: the ladies led by women: the men are banished to a distance of $\frac{1}{2}$ a mile to the N.' In the same year, another Victorian traveller, a Mr W. F. Campbell, had stayed in Granville during a tour of Normandy and was sufficiently impressed by this scene to make a sketch of it. Later his sketch was elaborated into a lithograph which was reproduced in a two-volume survey of what he had eaten, caught, said, thought and seen during his tour. It is unlikely that any but his friends ever read the book but he recorded this glimpse of life at a French coastal resort in 1848 [Plate 7].

Even without stopping to bathe at Granville, the Ruskins did not reach Coutances until eight in the evening. They stayed less than two days, leaving on the Wednesday, but in that short time Ruskin did far more work than he had done in such places as Falaise or Mortain where they had stayed longer.

For example, his diary notes record a description of the irregularly-sized pillars of the Cathedral of Notre-Dame, one of the finest in France, according to Murray. Nevertheless, Murray was at pains to point out the evidence on which he considered there was 'no reason to concede' the claim of the antiquaries of Normandy that it dated from the eleventh century.

Ruskin noted that the capitals were clumsy and of very poor workmanship 'as thus', with a sketch, and, in parenthesis, '(Note this principle—I have never thought of it before, that slender shafts must have spreading capitals)'. He made a careful sketch of one of the towers, 'if not the earliest, among the very early examples of the fully developed spire', and used it in his lectures on architecture in Edinburgh in 1853.

The Cathedral, as he described it to his father the day after their arrival, was 'full of interest but a little too much like Salisbury' and, he added, 'Our bill at St Michel was as you see *tout bonnement* and it includes George's board and lodging from Wednesday to Monday and we were perfectly comfortable as far as the *hotel* went—though the odour of the little street was—

outside—none of the sweetest—and the walks were somewhat monotonous. I am hurried to-day as I have a good deal to see in the Cathedral and the lovely environs. But it grows cold—if I sketch it must be from windows—the country is however still green and lovely.'

The next day he sent another letter, 'We leave this afternoon for St Lo. . . . This is a lovely place—like all the rest of Normandy that we have seen—hills and vales, and rocks breaking out here and there, and soft fields with avenues of trees between them, and lanes so loaded with blackberries that the hedge on each side looks like a piece of Florentine mosaic of bright black and red. But I am put out by the weather; it has grown so cold that I can only make rapid notes with greatcoat and gloves on—I hope there will be a change before I get to Rouen—but it does not much signify. I have pretty well examined this cathedral inside and out—there is not much detail about it—but it is marvellously interesting, a pure and complete example of the very earliest French Gothic. The rest of the town is quaint but dull, the view of the sea—Jersey and Brittany, superb.'

Effie, too, was impressed by the view. Writing from St Lo on the following Sunday, she described the 'long day's drive [to Coutances] and some parts very tiresome' and then, 'We had a splendid view from the top of the Cathedral seeing far over the sea and splendid sunset. The Islands of Chausey* full of Lime kilns sending up smoke looked exactly like a Volcano and on the other side farther off we saw Jersey.'

ST LO

Coutances had involved much work in the day and a half spent there. St Lo produced only one sketch and a few line

* Today 'the classical excursion of Granville' according to Michelin. 'You can land on the Grand Ile, the largest of this archipelago, whose wild character draws many tourists'. Michelin today is kinder to Granville than Murray was but even he finds the atmosphere 'somewhat austere'.

drawings of details but a full week was needed to complete them. It was an agreeable place to stay. 'A lovely place with beautiful walks and a fine broad deep river running past,' Effie wrote. 'We had a delightful sail the other night, George steering and John rowing; the high rocks and trees planted all the way up, and on the other side beautiful green fields with horses and cows, and a fine old Norman chateau among the trees, and the sun is so bright. I went afterwards to a bathing house and had a delightful warm bath and on the next night also; they are so clean; to-morrow I intend to have another. They put me in mind of home, only that the water here is ready at any hour and at any degree of heat. This inn is beginning to be very comfortable each day longer we stay in it; it is one of those where several diligences arrive in the day and where few people remain above one night, but as we remain on we get our things better and better.' They were fortunate as Murray had found the only inn, Le Soleil Levant, 'far from good and very dirty'.

Ruskin also found St Lo, like all Normandy, 'very wonderful for loveliness of lowland site'. He gave his father a detailed geological description, ending ' . . . while nearer the town the rocks are cut into terraced gardens—all bright with white and red roses and purple convolvulus—with peaches on the espaliers and grapes everywhere. However, for all this, beautiful though it be, I do not stop but for a little broken corner of the west front of the cathedral—quite unique in my experience and as far as I know—undrawn. There is a wooden house too—the richest I ever saw except the Abbaye St Armand at Rouen but alas this can be drawn no more, being placed thus . . . ' and then followed a sketch showing the wooden house being squeezed in by new houses on each side.

He followed Murray in calling Notre-Dame 'the cathedral'— one of the Hand-book's very few mistakes as it has never had that status. Murray conceded that the building was 'picturesquely situated' and had 'an imposing appearance' but on the whole he considered St Lo 'possesses no great attraction to the stranger'.

Ruskin closed his letter with a little lecture on economy to his father. 'It is a great luxury to me to receive your letters—still when there is nothing to tell me a long one every other day will be a better bargain than a line every day. I think the best way is for you to keep the letter by you until with each day's chat it is filled and so send it.'

The next day, Saturday, September 16, he wrote again: 'We think this place more and more lovely every day we stay, such walks I never saw except among mountains. . . . I have got a very beautiful subject here—but these architectural pieces take an awful time—I must stay Monday to finish it.' There followed another description of the town, ending, 'But I shall give you no idea of any of these places—the architecture takes me so long and I think it best at present to give myself to that and I cannot draw much for fear either of tiring or chilling myself. But I gain in strength every day—though Effie is amazed at my sensibility to draughts as much as I am at her weakness in anything like heat. But that will always remain with us. Effie might with reason feel a little dull here, for she is left alone more than half the day but she says she likes it very much—and we enjoy our afternoon's walk the more.'

Effie provided confirmation: 'John is taking a fine sketch of the façade of the Cathedral; he sits in a wool-comber's shop, not a very healthy or clean place. I go down occasionally and find him beside three women who comb the wool ready for spinning; they told me it was very unhealthy and it certainly was very dirty work for their aprons were covered quite black with the oil coming out of the wool. . . . I sit in the sun in the forenoon when John is sketching and draw and work by myself. John makes many lamentations being obliged to leave me for, as he says, such long dull hours and also after dinner but I am quite happy and I go for him at five and enjoy my walk till teatime very much. John is looking very strong and well and so am I and so is George if one may judge by the rumours of extraordinary breakfasts and dinners he sometimes gives us hints of having taken and I often see him when he goes out with me quietly munching a pear or some walnuts.'

George remembered nothing extraordinary about the breakfasts and dinners. 'St Lo, the chief town of the department of La Manche,' he recorded, 'has a fine cathedral also, with some very elaborate carving on the front, which Mr R. sketched a part of, the doing which occupied him three or four days. There were some nice walks by the side of the river, that I used pretty frequently, as well as having a little rowing now and then.'

At last the sketch was finished. 'A lovely morning—we are off at last—and shall be I hope at nine for [sic] Bayeux,' wrote Ruskin on September 21. 'All yesterday was taken up in finishing sketch and writing notes—the sketch has come out successfully even to its last scratch and I think you will like it. I never saw more graceful fragments than there are about this cathedral, and yet the top is so ugly that I believe had I came [sic] in by daylight, instead of night, I should have taken place in the Bayeux diligence without going to look at it. The weather is most lovely now—quite warm—windless and cloudless and I had sun every day for my sketch—which made it come out so well.'

In due course a part of the sketch on which so much time had been spent appeared as Plate II in the *Seven Lamps*. It seems that Ruskin liked it too much to leave it out altogether but had difficulty in finding an appropriate place. As there are some weeds growing in the carving of the door shown in the drawing, it was put opposite a page containing the passage '. . . there is not a cluster of weeds growing in any cranny of ruin which has not a beauty in all respects *nearly* equal to that of the most elaborate sculpture of its stones'. More than thirty years later, in 1880, Ruskin himself was puzzled by the apparent irrelevance of the drawing to the text and added a footnote to a new edition of the *Seven Lamps*: 'I do not see any reference to the intention of the opposite plate. It is a piece of pencil sketch from an old church at St Lo (I believe the original drawing is now in America,

7. The beach at Granville in 1848, from a lithographed drawing by W. F. Campbell

8. The new station at Harfleur, 1847

9. Detail of Notre-Dame, St Lo, by John Ruskin (pencil and brown wash, 19 × 14¼ inches.)

10. Charlotte Corday's house at Caen

11. Detail of St Sauveur, Caen, by John Ruskin (pencil and wash, $18\frac{5}{8} \times 13\frac{11}{16}$ inches.)

belonging to my dear friend, Charles Eliot Norton)* and it was meant to show the greater beauty of the natural weeds than of the carved crockets and the tender Harmony of both'. Neither then nor earlier had he noticed that, when etching the drawing on to the plate, he had forgotten to reverse it so that the reproduction shows the drawing in reverse [Plate 9].

Ruskin would have warmed to the burghers of St Lo of today. The town was obliterated in July, 1944, but there has been no question of restoring any part of the 'cathedral'. Instead, the ruins have been left as they were and a modern blue stone wall has been built to connect what remains of the chapel door, which Ruskin drew, with the remains of the tower to its right. It makes a moving group.

BAYEUX

The week's rest at St Lo came to an end and the Ruskins set off again by the 'mail light diligence' on Thursday, September 21. It was a short journey, only twenty-one miles, and a comfortable one. Ruskin reflected, in his letter that evening to his father, on the ease with which he could live like other people, eschewing all extravagance: 'I do not find certain economies at all painful, we do without a salon for instance with our two rooms—and save about four fr. a day—wine also—which does us no good—saves us another two or three—and the diligences go along so nicely that I am quite angry with myself for having thrown away so much money in posting on my Italian journey by myself.' All this was underlined and then, after dealing with family matters, he returned to the subject, underlining as before. 'All that I have to ask is that you will not labour on for us beyond your intended time—Every day that I spend in idleness and you in labour, I feel heavier and heavier on my conscience—

---

* Ruskin had, as he thought, given the drawing to Norton who had arranged an exhibition of Ruskin's drawings in America. It was later bought by Samuel Sachs and given to the Fogg Museum at Harvard University.

and I see that my notions of entire comfort and luxury are quite acceptable upon half the terms which you have given us—even travelling and living at expensive hotels sometimes—we are at present far within it.'

Bayeux itself had a mention only at the end of the letter: 'The cathedral here is superb—the finest early Gothic I have seen—but it is no use trying to draw anything unless I stopped a week—and I like Rouen better so I am going on [to] Caen today to save time—especially because Effie seems afraid of another long stop here and if I once begin on large paper, it is all up. Still there is nothing like what I got at St Lo. We shall take a look at tapestry and start at four D.V.'

Murray described Bayeux as 'a quiet and dull ecclesiastical city, with much the air of some Cathedral towns in England' and its chief ornament, the Cathedral, as a fine elevation 'though disfigured by a central cupola in a semi-Grecian style'.

If Effie wrote to her mother, the letter has been lost. Nothing is heard from her until ten days later by which time they had reached Rouen. The tapestry at Bayeux had not made a deep enough impression on her for her to remember it although Ruskin thought it 'the most interesting thing in its way conceivable—and delightfully visible and preserved'. By this time it was in the Public Library instead of the Hôtel de Ville where, according to Murray, 'it used to be unwound by the yard from a roller like a piece of haberdashery, and subjected to the fingers as well as the eyes of the curious'. Murray considered it a 'curious historical record' although it presented such anomalies as horses coloured alternately blue and red, and he reminded his readers that 'when Napoleon was meditating the invasion of England, he caused this tapestry to be transported from town to town and exhibited, on the stage of the playhouses, between the acts, to stimulate the spectators to a second conquest'. George evidently read and remembered his Murray for, after recording his impressions of the tapestry in his diary, he added 'Napoleon used it, in the last war, as a means of recruiting his army destined for the conquest of England, by sending it about the country and showing it to the peasantry to excite their passions.'

CAEN

They duly arrived in Caen on Friday, September 22, and stayed nearly a week. There was much to be done—including a number of letters to be written. Immediately on his arrival Ruskin wrote his father a very long letter dealing with family matters, and there was other correspondence to be answered. He then started on a detailed drawing of the church of St Sauveur [Plate 11], bigger (18 by 13 inches) than the drawing which had occupied him for so long at Falaise. 'If I get on with my drawing tolerably,' he told his father, 'I hope to get away from here on Thursday. There is a great deal in this place but I don't like it. One of its most interesting churches is quite inaccessible—in an hospital and nunnery [this was Ste Trinité in the Abbaye aux Dames] and another [St Etienne in the Abbaye aux Hommes] is too cold to stay in. The country round after what we have seen is quite ugly and the people are I think very bad, the utter corruption to the core of the system of life in this nation strikes me more and more—and I was equally disgusted yesterday with our own congregation of expatriated English—and their fat futile feeble clergy. One lives in the midst of decay—moral and material. . . . I shall probably not write tomorrow as I am very busy—not so in downright work as that I need time to put my thoughts together. I have now seen so much new and impressive.'

To add to the cold and the pressure of events at home (bearing down on Ruskin, no doubt, as his journey was drawing to its end), he now found that his budgeting had been at fault. 'I am sorry to find on casting up my accounts the day before yesterday,' he confessed, 'that our balance in hand of 355 francs will not take me beyond Rouen—Can I have another forty pounds to come home upon. I have been as economical as I could be except in 60 francs being uselessly paid to a *voiturier* at Abbeville when I was afraid of diligences and I have my accounts in better order this journey than I ever have before, all the bills made up together for reference. Effie has been buying more lace etc. here for which she is to pay me out of her allowance* when she gets home and she wants to buy some more things at Rouen—which something diminishes my present purse.

'I was interrupted by breakfast which brought your two pleasant letters of 23rd and 25th [Ruskin was writing on 27th] (Pray write whenever you have anything to say for no luxury is cheaper than one's letters even at the dearest) with the compliments on my economy—not very apropos to the beginning of this letter.† Indeed I can be far more economical yet without the least inconvenience to myself or to Effie and for that reason I believe I should never have any trouble in accommodating myself to my circumstances as long as these were known and fixed and not dependant on my own immediate exertions which would make me nervous. All my pleasures are cheap. I like walking better than a carriage—and a wooden chalet better than a fashionable hotel—a morning ramble better than an evening party—bread and butter better than meat—and water as well as wine so that as long as I need not sell any Turners, or my books, I am not afraid of any reduction of income—down to about 150 a year with less than which I do not think I should concede myself and Effie *à notre aise*—I don't mean to be philosophical—nor to say that I do not think my present income more desirable—but merely that if people would but live in peace and decency, and pull down no cathedrals, it would take a very considerable diminution of my income to make me lose my equanimity.'

Ruskin must have taken the unusual course of showing this letter to Effie for he added: 'Effie is afraid you will think her extravagant and begs me to say that she has bought only 80 francs—or 90 of things here and only will buy at Rouen things

* Of £25 a quarter, given to her by Ruskin.
† All the rest of the letter from this point is underlined.

to supply what will not last her till she gets to England. I am sorry my mother's cough is not gone but that I am certain there is something in the air this season—for though my cough has vanished ever since I left Abbeville—the least exposure to draught or chill is sure to bring back roughness in the throat in the morning: and I am obliged to leave much undone—in interiors and in draughty streets. I dare not stay in the Norman churches here for five minutes.'

Effie wrote a birthday letter to her brother George from Rouen on October 1 which tells all we know of her doings at Caen. 'John took me to the opera there, where we saw *Robert Le Diable* performed quite apropos being in Normandy . . . the boxes had more officers in them than any thing else and they are not to be compared to our officers in point of appearance or style, they have such a dirty, dark, unshaven look about them. . . . I saw the house of Charlotte Corday; there was nothing particular about it at all and her bedroom was like other French bedrooms.' [Plate 10]

This expedition irritated Ruskin exceedingly. 'Just as we were leaving Caen.' he wrote to his father the following Sunday from Rouen, 'the diligence at the door—but not the horses in— Effie asked me to walk down the street with her to see the house of Charlotte Corday—I at first refused—not being interested— not caring to appear interested—in any such character—but on her pointing out a description of it by M. de la Martine quoted in her Caen guide—I went with her to see how far the description was true—as I thought it might be the means of testing the man's character by a small thing—as indeed it proved. We found the number indicated—a thriving looking house—in the principal thoroughfare of Caen—leading straight from St Pierre to the only bridge over the river—and corresponding on a small scale to our Cheapside—leading as it were from St Paul's to London Bridge—and including the best shops and half the business of the town. Inquiring for the house [deleted] room we were shown into a narrow backyard—of the most commonplace

and utterly vulgar description—with a pump in it and as usual
a stone trough below for the water—evidently used every day
for "washing up". About every house in Caen not built in the
last twenty years has a winding stone staircase. So has this—
with rather a bold stone ornament at the top [a sketch the size
of a thumbnail]—the only thing in the house in the smallest
degree different from the "back airy" of any house in any town
of France. Now hear M. Lamartine.*

'"Dans une rue ecartié et déserte de la Ville de Caen" (he
begins, you see, with the Lie undecorated—the ornament comes
in as he proceeds) "on voit au fond d'une cour une antique
maison aux murailles grises, délavées par la pluie et lézardé par
'le temps'. Un puits à margelle de pierre—verdie par le mousse—
(you see, a pump in Mr. La Martine's hands is as valuable a stage
property as in Mr. Crummle's†)—occupe un angle de la cour.
Une porte étroite et basse, dont les jambages cannelés vont se
renouer au sommet en cintre, laisse voir les marches usées d'un
escalier en spirale qui monte à l'un supérieur. Deux fenêtres en
croisillons dont les vitraux octogones sont enchâssés en des
compartimentes de plomb (Very wonderful indeed that the
glass should be put in with lead. He might have added to the
interest by remarking the use also of putty—which is liberal)
éclairent faiblement l'escalier—(that is true enough and the
same is true to a greater extent of the Hotel d'Angleterre over
the way) et les *vastes*‡ chambres nues. (read—a middle sized bedroom with a dirty French bed—and an old woman in it). Ce
jour pâle imprime—(here comes the blue light of the French
painter) par cette vétusté et cet obscurité, à cette demeure, ce
caractère de délabrement, de mystère—et de mélancolie, que
l'imagination humaine aime à voir étendu, comme un *linceul*,

---

* The passage occurs in Lamartine's *Histoire des Girondins* (Vol. 6, page 190),
which was published in Paris in 1847. However, an earlier version had been published in a Paris newspaper, *La Presse,* of March 17, 1847, and this was reprinted
in 'Effie's Caen guide'. The two versions differ; for example, 'ecartié et déserte'
became 'large et populeuse' in the book and the past tense was used.

† *Nicholas Nickleby,* Chap. XXIV.

‡ *vastes* was omitted from the book version.

sur les berceaux des grandes pensées, et en les séjours des grandes natures."*

'Now, this is an unimportant passage about an unimportant thing but it seems to me to condemn the man utterly—it is lying of the most deliberate kind—lying in order to make a romance of murder—and an heroine of an assassin. I desire no more proofs of what the fellow is—the intention to deceive and to adorn is open and palpable and we are past the days now when histories are to be made [word obscured by postmark] Do not you fully agree with me and give him up at once—a cheat certainly—and considerably a fool besides.'

The strength of Ruskin's fury against Lamartine (never referred to in his published works) must have been based on the poet's political activities rather than his writings. Lamartine had become Foreign Minister in the provisional government which was formed on the abdication of Louis Philippe the previous March, having opposed the king bitterly. Before the end of the year Louis Napoleon was to be elected and Lamartine's political career finished but his anti-monarchical principles had evidently earned him the hostility of 'the staunchest Conservative in the British Islands' as Ruskin once described himself.[10] Ruskin's political views were complex but his attitude to the 1848 revolution was fairly well summarised in a letter written to W. H. Harrison, his friend and editor, from Calais on the way home on October 24: 'They say the king was a bad one, but better than none.'

---

* 'In a secluded and deserted street of the town of Caen there is, at the bottom of a courtyard, an ancient habitation, with grey walls rain-sodden and dilapidated by time. A fountain with stone brim, covered with moss, occupies one angle of the courtyard. A narrow low door, whose fluted lintels, uniting in an arch over the top, expose the worn steps of a winding staircase which leads to the upper storey. Two windows, with their octagonal panes of glass held in lead-work feebly light the staircase and the vast empty chambers. The misty daylight, by this antiquity and obscurity, impresses on the abode the character of vagueness, mystery and melancholy, which the human fancy likes to see spread as a shroud over the cradle of deep thoughts and in the abodes of imaginative minds' (from the English version of *History of the Girondists,* London, 1848, amended to meet the version quoted by Ruskin).

On the evening of the day that he wrote berating Lamartine, Sunday, October 1, Ruskin sat down again in Rouen to express his disgust with Caen to his father: 'Certainly I saw nothing good at Caen: I went to a Café to get my sketching regularly. The first day I went there, about eleven o'clock, in the upper room (sanded all over to conceal spitting) there followed me upstairs a party of 5 young men decently enough dressed—who sat down to drink beer, smoke, and play at cards. We all continued our occupations for about an hour and a half—when one of them having risen and come to the window to see what I was about, I put aside my drawing (after allowing him to see it) and began conversation by saying what a happy country France was, or must be as comparison of England, when the young men could afford the time and the money to spend in cafés from eleven to one—who with us would be compelled to work for their bread. He blushed considerably—and said it always happened more on Saturday which was a kind of holiday—"Then", I said, "on Sunday—tomorrow—of course you go to church"—"*Jamais*" he answered—but not in a spirit of bravado—on the contrary looking fidgetty and uncomfortable. "Never at all?" I said— "*Jamais*". "Then, I suppose you do not believe in God"—"Oh yes—certainly"—"Well, but then do not the priests tell you that you should go to church?"—"Ah, yes, but—*enfin ce n'est pas la coutume ici*"—"Well," I said—looking all the while very innocent and as if I asked for information—"then of course you say your prayers in the morning and when you go to bed". He looked round at this to his companions who were still drinking their beer but had left off their game at cards to listen: the question was received with a laugh indeed—but not an insolent one, as I expected. They seemed very much astonished —and partly puzzled to know what I was at, and partly amused at the evident discomfort of the person immediately addressed who replied hesitatingly "*Non—non—nous ne prions jamais— c'est-à-dire—enfin—on fait—la prière quand on est triste*"—"Well, but" I went on—"if you don't go to church—how do you know anything of the Bible—you can't live without ever hearing the Bible read—can you?"—This put him out again but he said "*Non, on ne lit jamais la Bible—on ne la connaît pas. On l'apprend déjà enfin—jusqu'à ce qu'on en est embêté. On n'y pense plus*"—"Well but" I said—"when you come to die—don't you want to know something about it?"—"*Mais oui—mais enfin—on ne pense pas*". He had got by this time so red in the face and so uncomfortable every way that I thought it best to press him no farther, but a day or two after—meeting him again—I ventured to suggest to him that he would find the Bible a very interesting book and that I thought he would find reading it quite as entertaining as card playing in the morning.'

But Ruskin must have known perfectly well what to expect in a Café for, had not Murray warned him? 'We have no equivalent in England,' Murray had written, 'and the number and splendour of some of these establishments, not only in Paris but in every provincial town, may well excite surprise. They are adapted to all classes of society, from the magnificent *salon*, resplendent with looking-glass, and glittering with gilding, the decorations of which have perhaps cost 4000*l.* or 5000*l.*, down to the low and confined *estaminets*, resorted to by carters, porters, and common labourers, which abound in the back streets of every town, and in every village, however small and remote. The latter sort occupy the place of the beer-shops of England, furnish beer and brandy, as well as coffee, and though not so injurious to the health and morals as the gin-palaces of London, are even more destructive of time: indeed the dissipation of precious hours by almost all classes in France produces as bad an effect on the habits of the people.' Unfertile ground for missionary activities and it is not surprising that we hear no more about them.

The sketching was a success—'Caen seems to me a most disagreeable place—though I have one of my best sketches as yet from it,' Ruskin wrote in the same letter. It was indeed one of his best sketches as can be seen from Plate 11, but he soon forgot where he had done it. 'At Caen—in the main Street (Not St. Pierre),' he inscribed it, whereas he must surely have enquired its name and been told it was called St Sauveur.*

Murray mentioned neither the church of St Sauveur nor the house of Charlotte Corday in the considerable space he devoted to Caen. Liveliness always meant more to him than mere antiquity (he described so many places as 'dull and lifeless') and he was able to say that 'notwithstanding the antiquity of Caen, its wider streets, its large central square, in which stands the statue of Louis XIV., and its houses of white stone, give it a more cheerful air than Rouen, though less enlivened by passing crowds'. In addition, Caen could offer 'the salubrity of its site, and the cheapness of house rent and provisions, which have caused our countrymen to settle themselves down here in a colony of 2,000 strong'. Finally, to show how he and Ruskin disagreed about Caen's merits, he added: 'The women of the lower and middle classes in Caen, and throughout a large part of La Basse Normandie, are finely formed, fully grown, and handsomer than in most other parts of France.'

Anything to do with William the Conqueror moved Murray deeply and he found space to tell the unhappy story of his end. He had already told how 'it was among the glowing embers of the houses and monasteries of Mantes, which he had remorselessly caused to be burnt, that William the Conqueror received the injury in his corpulent person, caused by his horse starting, which proved mortal a few days after at Rouen'. Tortured by the wound he 'repaired to the retired monastery of St Gervais in Rouen to die. His death-bed exhibited a melancholy example

* It had originally been called Notre-Dame de Froide-rue, and the name is recalled by the inscription drawn by Ruskin on the church's apse, 'Rue Notre-Dame'. This had been 'Rue St Pierre' and is now 'Rue St Etienne'. Ruskin gave the drawing to Norton, together with the St Lo drawing (see p. 55), both of which are now in the Fogg Museum. Before sending it to America he made an exact copy of it which is now in the Ruskin Galleries, Bembridge. The Fogg drawing was reproduced in *The Diaries of John Ruskin* (Oxford, 1958) and there described as a 'Detail of St Etienne'. St Etienne is Caen's greatest glory and the burial place of William the Conqueror—but Ruskin found it too cold for drawing.

of the vanity of earthly grandeur. Deserted by his own sons, when the breath was scarce out of his body, forsaken by friends and courtiers, and plundered by his servants, his body remained stripped and deserted, until the pity and charity of an unknown knight in the neighbourhood provided the funds necessary for the funeral; and he himself escorted the body to its last resting place at Caen.'

Now came the story of the funeral itself which was 'singularly interrupted, even within the precincts of the church, and before the service for the dead was concluded, by a cry from one of the bystanders, a man of low degree, who claimed the site of the grave, saying, that it occupied the place of his father's house, that he had been illegally ejected from it in order to build the church, and he demanded the restitution of his property. This claim, thus boldly made, in the presence of the dead monarch's son Henry, the chief mourner, being backed by the assent of the town's people, who stood by, was not to be denied or rejected, and the bishop was obliged to pay down on the spot 60 sous for a place of sepulchre for the royal corpse. Even then, it is related, that as the coffin was being lowered into the grave, it struck against some obstacle, fell and was broken into pieces, so that the corpse, ejected from its tenement, diffused so horrid a stench through the church, that the rites were hurried to a close, and the assembled priests and laity dispersed.'

CAEN TO ROUEN

Eventually the time came for the Ruskins to leave Caen. They could have travelled to Le Havre by boat and thence taken the English-built railway to Rouen which had been opened the previous year. There was a daily service 'starting as soon as the height of the tide allows them', according to Murray, and taking only four hours of which one-and-a-half were on the River Orne and two-and-a-half on the open sea. Ruskin wanted to see Honfleur, though, in spite of Murray's warning that it was a dull town 'and utterly without interest to the traveller, and moreover very dirty'. The little party therefore went by diligence from Caen to Honfleur, arriving very tired at midnight on Thursday, September 28.

Effie described it (from Rouen): 'The fish market at Honfleur is very curious, the old women sit with their fish on boards beside them on each side of a long street and a stream running down the middle. I never saw such a collection of fish, immense Oysters and skate, red mullet, Mackerel, eels, Herrings, and those horrid animals, dog fish all spotted over between a snake and a shark, I have not got their expressions out of my head yet.'

'From Caen', wrote George (where 'we stopped a week, Mr R. being busy sketching &c.'), 'we had a night's riding in the diligence, reaching Honfleur about ½ past 12, a.m. Abominably expensive hotel here opposite the pier, most exorbitant in their charges.'

In spite of his long letter to his father of the Wednesday, Ruskin still apologised for not sending another on Thursday. 'I could not write yesterday,' he wrote from Honfleur on Friday, 'I was so very busy finishing a drawing at Caen which I think is very pretty. To-day the boat leaves for Havre at one and I want to go out and see this place a little so I have only time for a line. Caen on the whole disappointed me exceedingly—there is too much stone in its neighbourhood and the houses are a great many of them white and commonplace and those which are curious are not very picturesque. The churches are wonderful— but spoiled in all manner of ways, whitewashed or restored—or half shut up. Bayeux would indeed have taken me a long time—if I had had time to give it but I had resolved to have a week['s] work for Rouen, and had none to give it.'

'I could not write yesterday,' Ruskin apologised again on the Sunday from Rouen, 'we had two very disagreeable days travelling and a wonderful church to see and I literally had not a minute—for I used the last six minutes given me by the diligence driver to run back to the church and count some arches which I had missed.'

It was at Caudebec that this occurred and Effie described how they reached the little town: '. . . next day after arriving at Honfleur we crossed the mouth of the Seine to Havre a most lovely sail of seven miles both coasts perfectly beautiful and a fine mild day. . . . Havre is the Liverpool of France [she was quoting from her Murray] but about half the size and has nothing interesting in it.* We got into the Railway at three and four miles later stopped at Harfleur [Plate 8] where you will recollect the first scene of Henry 5th opens with its siege.† The church built by him rises beautifully from among the trees. The town is sweetly situated in a Bay and put me much in mind of Rothesay. We next arrived at Yvetot and after sauntering about for two hours waiting for the Diligence, it came at six o'clock and took us to Caudebec on the Seine. I never saw a more beautifully placed town, the hills all along the banks of the river on both sides with lovely woods to the top just tinged with Autumn and the Seine so noble and deep running at the bottom and the Church quite wonderful—the stone work on the doors, which fortunately escaped the revolution, is so fine that it is almost impossible to draw it on paper and the painted glass windows inside are equally superb. It had a market in front yesterday and George and I went through to measure for curiousity two of the immense golden pumpkins that the people use for soup here. One was seven feet round and six broad and the other F 7—6 inches. That is pretty large for a fruit. It was very warm and I bought half a pound of black grapes for two sous. John was sketching the outside and I tried a little bit of painted glass

---

* Its way with bathers was surely interesting: 'There are no bathing-machines', wrote Murray, 'ladies are led out to a sufficient depth of water by the guide, who then seizes them by the shoulders, lays them on the surface of the water, and dips them by sousing their heads under water'.

† 'Or would you have chosen that your Prince Harry should never have played that set with his French tennis-balls, which won him Harfleur . . . ' wrote Ruskin later (*Works*, 27, p. 244), paraphrasing Act I, Sc. 2 of *King Henry V*.

inside but our labours were cut short by the diligence leaving at three for Yvetot, where we took the Railway and reached Rouen last night just as it was dark.'

George confirmed the beauty of Caudebec but not the almost incredible size of the pumpkins. 'We crossed the Seine to Havre, had a beautiful sail across of about an hour, it being very wide here. Havre is a large sea-port, and seemed very busy; we went on without stopping, by railroad to Caudebec, a prettily situated town, on the river Seine, which is here a noble river, reminding me of the views on the large American rivers [did he mean book illustrations?] the opposite side of the Seine, being here so flat, makes the river of a great width. There is an old church here which has some beautiful sculpture about it, the whole front is one mass of exquisite carving, the porches in particular; being Saturday it was market-day and a most excellent market it was, quantities of everything, beautiful black or white grapes, four sous (2*d*) per pound. We also saw some of the largest pumpkins I ever saw, perfect prodigies of nature. I took a measuring-line and measured them, but have lost their sizes, lots of fresh river fish as well as salt water; we left there by diligence and took the railroad to Rouen.'

'I expected only an interesting little village church,' Ruskin went on in the letter already quoted, but he must have expected rather more than that to have left the Havre–Rouen train at Yvetot, waited two hours for the diligence to Caudebec, put up with the Hotel du Commerce, which Murray warned was 'not very clean, but tolerable', and then be prepared to wait until three the next afternoon for the diligence back to the railway journey he had interrupted at Yvetot. The fact that Murray called Caudebec 'one of the prettiest little towns on the Seine' would scarcely have been enough, but Murray made it clear, in his description of the church, that it was more than an 'interesting little village church'. 'In fact,' wrote Ruskin, it had 'the richest portals—for deliberate workmanship on a small scale—I have yet seen: of a class however which it would have been in vain to have attempted drawing unless I had another week to spare.* Besides this the scene from the riverside is perfectly glorious: the river as broad as the Rhine but calm and glassy: with, on the opposite shore a plain as level as that of Marengo—and as vast†—with the long lines of poplars and masses of exquisitely grouped upright trees reflected stem for stem in the broad water: and on the Caudebec side—a sweeping theatre of hills as high, almost, as those of the Rhine but covered instead of vines with one mantle of forest. All that I used to say of French trees‡ is far below their deserving. Such romantic—far stretching—graceful successions of group and glade as cover the hills from here to Havre I never saw in any land. The mouth of the Seine, too—which we crossed from Honfleur to Havre on a sunny windless afternoon the day before yesterday, is a noble scene—not unlike the Gulf of Spezzia in its width and in the modulation of the hills on its shores—or perhaps I shall give it you more accurately by telling you to mix Gulf of Spezzia with firth of Forth. Havre itself, of course, I had planned to leave as soon as possible—expecting it to be like Liverpool—I was not sorry to leave it—but it was much more like Boulogne than Liverpool—it has a dock—certainly and some ships in it—and looks about as lively as Gloucester—or Stockton.

'Caen as I said disappointed me and I have—I hardly know why—a very disagreeable recollection of it. If you were to come to Normandy without me I should advise you not to go there at all but to go down as I did to Falaise and cross from Vire to St Lo. You would receive a far pleasanter impression of the country, and on the whole a truer, for the character of Caen is

* He had time to do the beautiful drawing now in the Fogg Museum (Plate 12.)

† The plain of Marengo is north of Genoa and Ruskin had written a poem on 'the sight of the Alps' from it. He was fascinated by Napoleon's Italian campaign, particularly the battle of Marengo.

‡ 'French trees are altogether unmatched; and their modes of grouping and massing are so beautiful, that I think, of all countries for educating an artist to the perception of grace, France bears the bell.' (*Modern Painters*, 1843, Pt. II, Sec. I.)

peculiar owing to its lying on a bed of Oolite—the celebrated Caen stone.'

ROUEN AGAIN

'. . . the narrow streets here are quite Paradise to me. . . . And Effie, as well as I, thinks that the people look much more respectable than at Caen.' So burst out Ruskin's enthusiasm for the city which had all that Caen lacked.

Murray called it 'the French Manchester' but his description hardly seemed to justify the comparison: 'The Seine, here more than 1000 ft. broad, forms a convenient port, accessible for vessels of 250 tons; and though the number of vessels is small, they add both to the picturesqueness and animation of the scene. Its banks are formed into fine broad Quais, and these are lined with handsome modern buildings, which have sprung up within the last 10 or 15 years, and serve as a screen to hide a rear rank of tottering timber houses, such as form the bulk of the city, and which previously extended down to the river side. Modern improvements and additions, indeed, have of late greatly detracted from the venerable and picturesque appearance of Rouen; but the changes are skin-deep, confined to its exterior, and the stranger has only to plunge into its almost inextricable labyrinth of streets to find enough of antiquity to satiate the artist or the most ardent lover of bygone times: although a law having been passed prohibiting the rebuilding of houses in wood, their number must diminish every year.' One or even two days was not enough for the visitor to see the things best worth observing. 'The distances from one quarter of the town to another are considerable, to say nothing of the want of pavement, the dirt, and the bad smells which he will have to encounter.'

12. Architectural study at Caudebec, by John
Ruskin (pencil and wash $12\frac{13}{16} \times 6\frac{3}{8}$ inches.)

13. Part of the entrance to the south transept, Rouen Cathedral from a daguerreotype in Ruskin's collection, showing the building on the left in Plate 4

Ruskin continued: 'We went to the protestant service this morning and to vespers in the afternoon in the cathedral—which after all we have seen—comes upon me finer than ever—the portal is such a vast and infinitely filled piece of beauty that I have never yet been able to take it into my mind—or comprehend it—or conceive it when I was away from it. It seemed quite new to me again this evening and gave me a sensation like St Mark's place [Venice]. I am going to devote this week wholly to it, and if I cannot draw it, at all events I hope to know something about it and understand it a little. But if the weather is tolerable—Stay—an idea—I will hire an hackney coach even if it rains as I used to do at Naples, and I hope to get a beautiful finisher of my Norman sketches—or—if not—at all events a sufficient remembrance of this—my ideal as it has always been of Gothic proper—and the scene of my fondest dreams—after Venice—ever since I was fifteen.'

But there was no need for the hackney coach. 'Rouen is much gayer than before when we saw it,' wrote Effie in her birthday letter to her brother George on October 1, the day after their arrival, 'and I suppose it is the weather, for it is quite lovely and warm and I am wearing my pale green and pink silk dress which I had turned at Caen and it looks quite new. The Opera is also open every evening.'

In this atmosphere Ruskin's work went on, uninterrupted by anything except anxiety over the non-arrival of his father's letters. He then found, either that he had neglected to inform the postmaster of his arrival, or that it had not been recorded. Whatever the cause, Mr Ruskin's letters of September 26 and 27 arrived in Rouen only to be forwarded to Falaise in accordance with the instructions left two months previously. From Falaise, again following the instructions left in August, they were sent to Avranches and thence to Bayeux and Caen, and finally back to Rouen. Astonishingly enough, all this took but a week and on October 4 the letters were in Ruskin's hands. The important letter—containing the money, however, was not among them 'and being now reduced to my last ten pounds (and one louis),' he wrote, 'which I have benevolently divided with George, I look with some anxiety for the coming of supplies.'

The supplies came, of course—they always had and they always would. 'I have to-day your letter of the third,' Ruskin wrote on the 5th, 'with the twenty pounds—which came just in time and the announcement of the missing letter of the 30th with 40 pounds which I immediately enquired for but got nothing but shrug of shoulders from postoffice people—who however said they supposed it had gone to Falaise and would be back in due time from its tour of Normandy. I received from the same tour a letter from Richard Fall* dated 25th Sept but being postmarked Boulogne 29th Sept, Rouen 30th, Falaise 1st and 2nd Oct, Avranches 2nd Oct, Bayeux 4th, Caen 4th—accordingly if my money letter did not each Boulogne till the first it will be the day after to-morrow before it arrives here. I have no doubt it will come in time and I have plenty to go on with but it is too bad of the postoffice people here to send away a letter on Monday just after being told we were here. The weather is now beautiful and I am getting on with my sketch.'

Whether the post office deserved blame for their original error or praise for their redemption of it, they were now giving Effie a few extra days of happiness by delaying a letter with bad news in it. To save postage it was the practice of her parents to send their letters to Mr Ruskin for enclosure with his (unless there was anything in them they did not want him to read, as occasionally was the case) and on October 6 Ruskin received a letter (forwarded from Caen) which had taken a week to arrive. It enclosed a letter for Effie 'containing', as Ruskin informed his father, 'news which I had not the heart to give her this morning: she had been unwell and was just recovering to a day of enjoy-

---

* A school-friend of Ruskin's with 'no particular tastes. . . . We got gradually accustomed to be together, and far on into life were glad when any chance brought us together again.'

ment. I will give her them this evening when the shock will be less. She loved her aunt Jessie exceedingly.'

Aunt Jessie, who had died, was the wife of Effie's mother's brother, Melville Jameson, and both Effie and her mother had been devoted to her. Effie's first duty was to write a letter of sympathy to her mother and, a few days later, to consult both her parents on the matter of mourning. 'John sympathises with me most kindly', she wrote to her father on October 10, 'but he did not know her and could not be supposed to understand her. He, like you Papa, has a great dislike of mourning and did not wish me to wear more than half mourning. I had curiously bought the enclosed dress [sic] the other day, being the fashionable colour, which will be very useful to me with black for the above purpose, but as I told him that my feelings, and that I thought Melville's also, would be hurt if I did not wear it, as I remember he was always very particular about poor Jessie's wearing proper mourning; tell Mama I am getting a black silk dress and black lace bonnet which John is pleased with and wishes me to do whatever is right. Now I would be obliged to my mother to tell me what she thinks right and I will do it. . . . John is quite well and making some beautiful sketches here. I am trying to do the painted glass, which pleases him very much; we are extremely happy together and have been married half a year to-day.'

John was indeed well and happy. 'I get on with my drawing slowly though well,' he reported, 'the weather is everything I could wish. Every hour I spend in this place gives me more delight and wonder.' And, as a postscript, 'the money letter should arrive in due course from Caen to-morrow morning.' It arrived just as expected and the slight irritation that each had felt with the other, due to missing letters, was dissolved. 'I don't wonder at your being annoyed, but . . . ' and Ruskin explained what had happened. Then he went on: 'My sketch is only two thirds done—if so much, and I work as hard as I can not to hurt myself. But it is physically impossible to make a drawing of any size with any degree of attention to details in less than a week and this Rouen drawing is on *two sheets* joined.* I never work before breakfast but sit at it from ½ past nine to twelve each day which is as much as I can do of such work. In the afternoon I cannot sit in the place, the sun being full on it, so I go and make general observations—take sections etc.—and the more I study the more awestruck I am. I think this cathedral may stand second to that of Florence and the two squares before its west and south doors second to St Mark's Place and the Piazzetta.'

As if to mark the closing of the rift, Mr Ruskin then sent a totally unexpected extra fifty pounds. His son promised to take care of it 'and not let my sudden rise from a capital of 10 francs to one of 110 pounds turn my head. The bankers will get quite respectful: they were wonderfully cool and rude at first but have been giving five hundred francs worth of additional politeness every bill I draw: and the old spectacled gentleman who wanted very much to charge me a commission which he had no business with—seeing Effie sitting on a post while I was making a memorandum at the cathedral doors, went so far as to come out to ask her in to a chair and a glass of water—source perhaps.' He then went on to discuss the livery of a recently bought family Brougham and ended with elaborate professions of the gratitude he felt towards his father but so rarely expressed. Then, as a postscript, he added a description of vespers in the Cathedral. But there was no need for his father to worry: they had been to a Protestant service in the morning and 'vespers are very nearly our English evening service magnificently chanted'. (No doubt he heeded Murray's plea on behalf of the twenty-five resident English ministers in France: 'With few exceptions the stipends are very small, and English visitors availing themselves of the privilege and benefit afforded by these places of worship should remember that they are in duty bound to contribute, according to their means, to the support of the

* The drawing has disappeared; Plate 4 was drawn in 1868.

establishments and their ministers'.) Finally there was the post-postscript which would please Mr Ruskin most: 'I propose D. V. leaving this—though it will still be with deep regret—on Saturday [October 14]. You may write me therefore here as late as Thursday with perfect safety. After that to Beauvais till Monday, and, on Tuesday or Wednesday to Amiens where I shall probably spend [until] Sunday, reaching Calais I trust on the Monday and home Tuesday if boat crosses or early on Wednesday if later.'

Three days later, on Wednesday, October 11, he renewed his apologies for his delayed homegoing. 'I have not been able to get away,' he wrote, 'it would be quite a sin to leave my sketch here incomplete—with the chance of the cathedrals being knocked down before I can return again—for I don't think by all I can see or hear, that things will keep quiet—of that however —viva voce is better [did he think of his letters being censored?]. It is a sad thing to see so many people drunk in the morning as one does now—there were two fellows reeling about under the cathedral porch this morning—I am getting very strong impressions of human vice and folly here—but there are bright spots now and then—and the pleasant interlude with one or two of the more respectable people—shopkeepers or dressmakers— or protestant clergymen—something softens what would otherwise be horror and scorn and pity all mingled into one shade. . . . I am very anxious to get home now as I know you must be to see us but I think you would be vexed if I left my work undone—We are both quite well. Effie is recovering from her late shock and we are very happy.'

A note from Effie, or possibly the end of a letter from her, reads: 'I am very grateful for the money and it enables him to get some fine Daguerreotypes* and me, Alas! to get some mourning for my Aunt. John and I will certainly come to Denmarkhill to tell you our news before going to Park St. I

* One of them, found among Ruskin's possessions at Brantwood, is reproduced in Plate 13.

have to beg you to excuse this dull note and to ask you to present my best love to Mrs Ruskin and yourself from your affectionate Daughter, Effie. C. Ruskin.'

Mr Ruskin needed reassurance of an early homecoming for he was evidently becoming impatient. 'You say if Normandy takes three months what will Italy take,' Ruskin replied on Thursday, October 11. 'This is so far indeed a true rule of three—but my stay in Normandy has been lengthened by my fear of not being able to get abroad again soon, or perhaps, ever to see some of the finer things in their present state again. They are defacing so much everywhere that I thought it foolish to run the chance of losing my study of this cathedral porch. I have never till now had any opportunity of really fathoming this architecture of France: and I have had great difficulty in doing so even in the long time I have had. You cannot imagine the intricacy of its arrangements. . . . ' and there followed an account, illustrated with sketches, of the difference in section between French and Italian columns. Finally, another reassurance: 'We are going to make a dash at home as soon as we leave this. We hope to spend the Sunday after next at Calais and to reach home Monday or Tuesday and when I say "hope" I mean, we have determined to do so—D. V.—come what may of temptation on the road.'

The temptation on the road was to be deferred a little longer. On Sunday, October 15, they were still in Rouen, Ruskin writing, 'I find myself still under the shadow of the cathedral here, though without altering at all our plan of reaching home. I have only given up all idea of more than *seeing* Gisors and Amiens—all that I have done here would have been nearly useless if I had not in some sort finished it. We hold to reaching Dessein's hotel [in Calais] on Saturday evening next and if you and my mother, or you alone, could come there to meet us—it would be very happy: you might leave Caroline and her husband* in possession of Denmark Hill for two nights. I hope you

* Count and Countess Béthune (*see* p. 21).

will do this—as—though I am exceedingly glad to hear that we are to have the pleasure of meeting them, I should like to have a quiet evening with you first. Unless unavoidably hindered, we will not fail you at Dessein's on Saturday next and as this letter will I hope reach you on Tuesday, you will have time, if you can come, to write to Dessein to ask for our old rooms: and to send a line to me at Amiens telling we may expect you. I am sure it would do my mother good to have this little change, and there could be no rudeness I think in leaving the Countess until Monday as they can give us so much time afterwards. For the rest, I am very glad they are to be there as it is right that Effie should see something of them and, although she dreads the introduction just now, I am sure she will be very happy with the Countess.

'Best thanks for the wine which I hope to keep until it gets as picturesquely dusty on the outside as the Porch of this Cathedral. I was going to ask the Bishop for leave to wash it but on cleaning some little bits experimentally, I found the stone behind white and soft, so that its effect would have been quite raw and new, and I prefer leaving it as it is although its carvings are literally in many places choked up two inches deep with an accumulation of soot, cobweb and dust washed from above and drifted from below.

'I still feel that I leave this place unseen; this is partly however owing to my very slowness in taking in: I cannot grasp it. Every time I walk into the square it is new to me. Still I verily believe that I now know more about it than any English architect, and than most French, and I have improved in my drawing these three months considerably: the different style of Gothic quite beat me at first and still it does in a great degree. I have not once succeeded in giving the *true* effect of a highly ornamental flamboyant niche, though I think I have come nearer it than most people.

'We had the Protestant clergyman and his son to dinner yesterday—such good nice people. . . . ' And so Ruskin ended his last letter home,* folding it, as always, and writing on the exposed back of the folded paper 'J. J. Ruskin, Esq. Denmark Hill, Camberwell, London, Angleterre'.

Effie had not written to her mother for a fortnight and had much to tell her in her letter of Sunday, October 15: 'John had so much to do here that we could not leave yesterday as proposed; therefore we only intend spending a day at Gisors, Amiens, Beauvais, and getting to Calais on Saturday evening, crossing to Dover if weather permit on Monday and arriving at Denmarkhill the same day, so you will be so good as to send my letters there till I tell you. The Count and Countess Béthune are to be tomorrow with Mr and Mrs R. from Ireland to remain a month, this is rather disagreeable, for John wanted to get a quiet chat with his parents and I wished to arrive quietly, spend two days at Den. Hill and go to Park Str. as I feel far from inclined to meet strangers at present, and John has written asking his father and Mother to leave their guests and meet us at Calais: the French could easily take care of themselves, but I think it would be very absurd coming such a distance in this cold frosty weather although I have not said so to John since the letter is gone.'

It was indeed a preposterous idea and nothing more was heard of it. Effie went on to describe the Vespers they had attended in the Cathedral and added: 'George and John were very much struck with the service and when we came out we walked up and down looking at the noble Cathedral lit up by the flowermarket lamps. George found Architecture rather cold at night especially on smelling the fine roast chesnuts from the fires at the fruit stalls and soon after I found he had been buying some.' Ruskin had told his father, in his letter discussing the decoration of the new Brougham: 'All this last week I have sent George to the Abbaye St Amand to trace the paintings of

---

* Or, at any rate, the last to have been preserved. It is hard to believe he did not write again during the ten days of the journey home.

flowers on the wainscot. He has got about 16 panels: most beautiful.'*

Effie continued: 'The other evening John and I were kept awake till one in the morning by noise in the Place below and carriages rolling accompanied by a troop of Cavalry. Next morning we found they were conveying the insurgents of Rouen in the June affair† to Caen to be tried and amongst them were a number of women singing "Mourir pour la patrie". The Ouvriers here were so displeased that they crowded the streets till that hour and they hate the soldiers and upper classes so much that the latter will soon not be able to go out after dusk. The Revolution is teaching the people a bitter lesson. Into all the shops we go the poor people complain of their own losses, and the workmen they can no longer employ are in such distress and they all say they were quite contented with the Government and that the Revolution was caused by people who had nothing to lose.' She ended with a description of the evening with the Protestant clergyman and, finally, the usual family matters. At last the stay in Rouen had come to an end and there would be a letter waiting for her, she supposed, at Gisors.

THE JOURNEY HOME

It is not easy to understand the reasons for Ruskin's choice of his route home. He had always intended to make Gisors the first stopping place after Rouen and had arranged for letters to be sent there some time previously—too long ago, in the event, as the stay in Rouen became prolonged. Yet he could not have

---

* This is hard to explain as Murray described the Convent of St Amand as 'recently pulled down' and, as far back as 1836, Gally Knight, to whom Murray had acknowledged some indebtedness, wrote that it was 'half demolished'. The façade is now in the Rouen Museum.

† The workers had rioted June 23–26, 1848, in protest against the proposed abolition of the national workshops which had been established to help the unemployed.

expected much of the parish church from Murray's description of it: 'it presents a singular combination of styles, and an abundance of uncouth sculptures . . . the sculpture is of the latest style of French florid Gothic, and much overladen with ornament.' Nor did he find much, for Effie wrote from Gisors, 'The day is cold and raining and I am not going out as John says there is nothing worth seeing.' Gisors was on the high road from Paris to Rouen and from Paris to Dieppe but there was no railway to it from any direction. Moreover, the railway from Rouen to Paris had diverted much of the traffic from it and the diligences along the high road had been withdrawn.

The Ruskins arrived at midnight on Monday, October 17, and were to leave at three o'clock the next afternoon. Effie spent the morning on her letter home and they then left for Beauvais.

Both Ruskin and George knew Beauvais, having stayed there three years earlier in 1845 on Ruskin's first tour abroad without his parents. Its cathedral had been built with the intention of surpassing that of Amiens but the money had run out and it was never finished. In this it was not alone among the cathedrals of northern France and Murray quoted the old tag that to find the perfect cathedral you would have to take the choir of Beauvais, the portal of Rheims, the nave of Amiens and the tower of Chartres. Ruskin had noted in his 1845 diary that Beauvais had disappointed him.

The Ruskins must have stayed in Beauvais, however, on the Tuesday and Wednesday, leaving for Amiens on Thursday the 19th. Ruskin had originally intended to reach Amiens on the Tuesday or Wednesday and stay until Sunday. He had been there with his parents in 1844 and found the front 'disjointed and incongruous'. In later years he was to revisit it many times and to form a very different opinion. But on this occasion he was not to see it at all.

It was but a short distance from Beauvais to Clermont-sur-Oise and from there they would be able to take the Paris–Amiens train for the sixty-seven miles to Amiens. When they arrived at the station at Clermont they found they had three hours to wait for the train to Amiens. The train to Paris, though, was just about to leave and Ruskin took one of the few impetuous decisions of his life. He decided to get into it.

'We arrived [in Paris] safely', wrote Effie from Calais on the following Monday, 'having great trouble at the Railway before we could get our trunks which were opened, everything examined. I should think George was an hour with the Police, they are so afraid of gunpowder coming into Paris at this time. We found very comfortable rooms and everything nice. Next morning we got a carriage and drove to the Louvre where John showed me his favourite pictures which I enjoyed very much. We walked to the end a long way and coming back met a M: Duodoin,* an artist of John's acquaintance. The Gallery was full of artists copying the Pictures. We then went and had some lunch, tried hard to get tickets to get into the Chamber of Deputies, for which one pays a pound or two of our money, but every ticket was sold and it is full every day just now. We then went a drive through the streets where the fighting was worst and where the Archbishop was shot†. They are going to put up a monument to him in Notre Dame which, by the way, I thought very little of after the fine Norman Churches. The Houses have still the marks of the terrible conflict, although mended with neood anw wd some end of streets in the

Page 81, line 24 should read:

mended with new wood and some ends of streets in the

only saw two people pass, a great many shops are shut and I did

* Dieudonné. Ruskin had met him as a youth in Florence and taken lessons from him.
† In June, 1848, Monseigneur Affre, Archbishop of Paris, had been shot (probably accidentally) while trying to mediate between the Government and the rebels in the Faubourg St Antoine.

not see a single well-dressed man or woman the whole day above
the rank of shop keepers and we were only in a barber's who said
that all the honest tradesmen were nearly ruined. I saw no nice
things, the people hanging about the streets have an air of
distrust and vice plainly written. I never saw anything so triste
but I am very glad to have seen it although I should rather not
pass the winter there. John said he could not have believed
Paris could have been so changed.'

They stayed at the Hotel Meurice in the Rue de Rivoli where
the Ruskins had always stayed. Murray described it as 'a
comfortable and well-managed house, much frequented by
Americans'. (Murray wrote very little about Paris on the grounds
that 'Galignani's Paris guide appears so good as to relieve the
Editor of this work from the necessity of entering into any
description of the French Capital at present'.) Effie had described
the sudden change of plan: 'We found we had to wait three hours
for the Amiens train: the Paris train was just leaving to be in
Paris at Meurice's in an hour and a half'. It must have taken
longer than that, though, as the railway journey alone was over
forty miles.

They went to the theatre in Paris, although Effie did not
mention it. Could she have felt a little guilty at doing so while
she was in mourning for her aunt? There is no doubt that she
went, though, for George afterwards noted: 'When at the
station [Amiens] we found that the train didn't leave for $1\frac{1}{2}$ hour
[Effie's 'three hours' was a more immediate, so more reliable,
record] so changed our route and went to Paris, got in about 5
and in the evening went to the Italian Opera, saw Lucia di
Lammermoor, Lucia Madme Persiani, beautiful singing'.*
Moreover, Ruskin made the following note in faint pencil at the
end of his architectural notebook—not his diary, which ends at
Rouen, but in one of the little books which he filled with technical
notes and a host of detailed sketches, many of them in colour:

---

* It was at the Théâtre des Italiens. Donizetti, who had died in April, 1848,
wrote *Lucia de Lammermoor* specially for Fanny Persiani (1812–1867) in 1835.

	Frs		
In hand Paris			
Friday 250 + 400		650	
Paid Effie hair	82		
Carriage all day	18		
Valet de Place⎱			
lost money ⎰	23		
Theatre	25		
Carriage to railway	4		
Bill & waiters at P.	93	10	
	245	10	
Fares to Amiens	42	12	
	287	12	

650	
287	12
362	18

'Paid Effie hair frs 82'? What could she possibly have had done to her hair? Even a visit to a doctor to find the cause of its falling out could hardly have cost as much. A switch or some other form of false hair to replace the loss is the only plausible explanation. With this and the 'lost money' (which must have been some 18 francs as Murray tells us the *valet de place* would have accounted for only 5 francs out of the 23) it had been an expensive jaunt. Effie, however, had earned a little diversion: she had had two months of Norman churches and still faced the dreaded meeting with the Béthunes. 'The Count and Countess arrived last Wednesday. It is quite a shame of them not looking after their Tenantry at home and exerting their influence,' she wrote with some asperity.

Ruskin does not seem to have enjoyed Paris very much. He wrote to W. H. Harrison from Calais on the following Tuesday, October 24, a long letter describing the state of France as he had found it during his tour: '... I have been in Paris for two days; it had always a black, rent and patched, vicious and rotten look about its ghastly faubourgs: but to see—as now is seen—all this gloom without the meanest effort at the forced gaiety which once disguised it—deepened by all the evidences of increasing—universal—and hopeless suffering: and scarred by unhappy traces of a slaughterous and dishonourable contest—is about as deep and painful a lesson—for those who will receive it—as ever was read by vice in ruin. But the melancholy thing is the piteous complaining of the honest inhabitants—all suffering as much as the most worthless, and not knowing what to do or where to look. . . . However, it is to be remembered that we were in Paris at what would, under any circumstances, have been a dull period; and that we went into its worst quarters. Its best are however nearly deserted, and in the gardens of the Tuileries, where I have seen the people of an afternoon thronged like ants, and mobs of merry children skipping under and about the trees, we counted the passers-by by twos and threes, and saw nothing dancing but dead leaves'.[11]

At seven o'clock in the morning of Saturday, October 21, they left the city where they had seen 'nothing dancing but dead leaves'. They went by railway to Amiens where they arrived at eleven, changed trains and continued, via Arras and Douay (Douai) to Lille.

'At Lille,' Effie wrote later from Calais, 'we stopped to walk through the town and have a little dinner, then from there to Calais, accompanied the whole way by the National Guards and two Vivandiers who looked very nice in their nice costume and little brandy chests tied round their waists.'

There was no way of covering the sixty-eight miles from Lille to Calais except by diligence and why they ever chose this route home is inexplicable. They had to stop at Amiens to collect their letters for, until they had them, they could not know whether or not Mr Ruskin (and perhaps Mrs Ruskin) were on their way to Calais to meet them. The natural thing would have been for them to do so and then continue by a later train to Abbeville and Boulogne by the new extension. If they still wanted to continue to Calais instead of crossing from Boulogne, after they knew Mr Ruskin was not meeting them, they would have had only a twenty-two-mile diligence journey as against the sixty-eight miles from Lille. Instead, they sent George to collect the letters at Amiens (with most unfortunate results which they were only to learn later) while they themselves went straight on to Lille by another train.

Ruskin was evidently determined to cross from Calais and not Boulogne. In the first place, the shorter sea crossing might encourage his father to meet him there and, when that reason no longer prevailed, he no doubt wanted to show Effie the Calais which, unlike Murray, he so loved.

Murray so detested Calais that he would not even give it credit for providing the shortest sea crossing. It took two hours, according to him, whether you went by Dover–Boulogne, Folkestone–Boulogne or were foolish enough to go by Dover–Calais. This is hard to believe, and Murray must have been glossing over the difference, small though it may have been. He noted with satisfaction that 'the preference now given to Boulogne has diminished the custom of the hotel-keepers' of Calais, but he quickly added that 'this circumstance leads them to indemnify themselves by an increase of prices'. He quoted an English traveller of the time of James I who described Calais as 'a beggarly, extorting town; monstrous dear and sluttish', and commented, 'In the opinion of many, this description holds good down to the present time.'

Ruskin felt very differently. 'Calais', he had written, '—the busy—the bustling—the—I had almost said the beautiful, for beautiful it was to me, and I believe to every one who enters it as a vestibule. See Calais and you can see no more, though you should perambulate France from the Atlantic to the Mediterranean. It is a little France, a miniature picture but not the less a resemblance. Stand on the pier and look round you. The sky is a French sky, it is a very turquoise, the sea is French . . .'[12] and so on and on and on. And in 1851 he was to write: 'Every traveller must love Calais, the place where he first felt himself in a strange world'[13] (this was in the course of describing Turner's *Fort Rouge, Calais*, which Turner 'saw after he had been home to Dessein's, and dined and went out again in the evening to walk on the sands, the tide being down'). Dessein's Hotel even came into an execrable poem Ruskin had written when sixteen years old.

So it was at Dessein's that Effie found herself on Saturday night after discovering that all their luggage had been left behind at Amiens. 'George was sent to the Post,' she wrote, 'for letters, to come on by next train. He thought we had our trunks and we thought he had. We had not a minute to see about them and on arriving here at eleven o'clock on Saturday night we found we had nothing with us except my dressing box which I fortunately always take charge of myself. We were very tired having been on the road 15 hours, nearly all the time on the Railway.'

George's version of the affair was: 'At Amiens the train stopped 20 min. and I was sent to the Post Office for letters; ran there and back, and arrived just in time to see the tail of the train rapidly getting out of sight. Waited about three hours then went on by next, going round by Lille, Valenciennes, found out when I arrived at Calais that the luggage had been left at Amiens; sent word back next morning as it was past 11 and too late for that night; all Sunday past, no luggage came, obliged to go out and buy some things for myself and Mr R. got it all safe on Monday.'

Murray spelt the hotel 'Dessin' and noted it as 'very good'. He added, 'the bedroom in which the author of *A Sentimental Journey* slept is till marked Sterne's room; and that occupied by Sir Walter Scott is still ticketed with his respected name.' Ruskin would have approved the tribute to Scott, whom he revered, having been 'brought up' on him, better than to Sterne whom he thought little enough of. Sterne, though, had done more to deserve the compliment of a room named after him for he had immortalised the 'Monsieur Dessein' of eighty years before by making him a principal character in *A Sentimental Journey*.

It proved difficult to get away from Dessein's. 'We went to the Steamer this morning at eight in a heavy shower,' Effie was writing on Monday, October 23, 'and found it with two others packed full of the 11th Legion of National Guards going to London for an excursion. If the weather had been good it would have been very nice. There are an immense number of them, enough to take Dover. They came from Paris on Saturday in order to present the national Guard here with colours and yesterday they had a grand fête. The Town was one scene of bustle from end to end, the streets all decorated and the regiments walking in procession, each man with a bouquet of flowers in his coat and another on the end of his bayonet. . . . From that circumstance we are forced to stay till tomorrow. I will post this at Dover so that you will know if we arrive safely.'

But on Tuesday it was no better. In the evening Effie added a postscript to her Monday's letter: 'We tried hard to get across again this morning but, as yesterday, found five hundred Guards going over and the boats filled. It was raining besides. It was a fine sight to see them go off, all singing together and waving their hats. . . . ' (Effie was always attracted by a soldier in uniform and a description of their uniform and appearance followed.) 'We think it best to go over at ten with the Mail, a nice boat and I suppose no passengers. We shall be tired enough when we do reach Dover at midnight and I fancy I shall be ill enough, but we don't like staying here.'

The oncoming winter must have increased the anxiety of all of them to be home. According to George, 'Sunday and Monday, Calais was very busy fraternizing and feasting with the National Guards from Paris, who embarked for London on Monday. During the procession I went to the English Church, buttoned up to the throat like a Polish refugee.' This was George's last memory of the tour: 'Saw four of Napoleon's old

Guard in the procession, two minus a leg each, one an arm, the other perfectly whole; they had lots of bouquets given them.'

Finally the National Guard were all embarked* and the civilians were allowed on board. On October 27, 1848, Effie was able to head her letter 'Denmark Hill' and tell of the last adventure of the tour: 'We left Calais on Tuesday night at eleven in a beautiful little screw steamer. There were no passengers in the Cabin but four National Guards with whom before starting I had an hour's very amusing talk. They went away and I was left in sole possession of the Ladies Cabin painted all round and Marquetries work like your drawing room chairs. I lay down, shut my eyes and arrived at Dover at one in the morning. John and I were the only two in the Boat not ill. We had to pass over a long narrow ladder into another ship to land in a pour of rain and the deep sea underneath. The deck was so slippery that the men could scarcely hold it [the ladder] and when one of the N. Guards was on it it slipped and if he had not been caught he would have been in the water. If the ladder had been so [ladder drawn diagonally] it would have been nothing in comparison, but it was so [drawn horizontally] and we were obliged to creep along on hands and knees and the ladder shaking. It makes me shudder to think of it yet. I do not know how I got over but there was nothing for it but going or sleeping on board all night.'

And so, after four months, John and Effie Ruskin left France behind them. The masons went on knocking down the churches. The railways went on spreading at the expense of the diligences. Murray went on recording it in detail. Other travellers were eagerly awaiting the next edition of his *Hand-book*.

---

* They visited the Lord Mayor and stayed in London until the following Friday. Before leaving, they wrote to *The Times* 'to thank the inhabitants for their cordial and truly fraternal reception'. *The Times* regretted only that they had 'come upon us unawares' or their reception would have been even more cordial.

SOURCES

Ruskin's letters, with the exception of the one on p. 27, are in Yale University Library, New Haven, Connecticut. Effie Ruskin's letters, John Hobbs's diary and Ruskin's letter quoted on p. 27 are in the Pierpont Morgan Library, New York. Ruskin's diaries and some of his notebooks are in the Ruskin Galleries, Bembridge, Isle of Wight, and other notebooks in Princeton University Library.

Extracts from some of Ruskin's letters have been quoted in the Library Edition of his *Works*, edited by E. T. Cook and Alexander Wedderburn (George Allen, 1903–12), referred to below as *Works,* and extracts from some of Effie Ruskin's letters in *The Order of Release* by Admiral Sir William James (John Murray, 1947). Otherwise the material used has not hitherto been published.

1. *Effie in Venice,* Mary Lutyens, John Murray, 1965, p. 19.
2. *Works,* Vol. 8, p. xxviii.
3. *Works,* Vol. 35, p. 106. (Vol. 35 of the *Works* is Ruskin's autobiography, *Praeterita,* 1885–9. Other quotations from it are not separately noted in these source notes.)
4. *Effie in Venice,* p. 315.
5. *Works,* Vol. 8, p. xxix.
6. *Works,* Vol. 3, p. 210.
7. *Sixty Miles from England,* Simona Pakenham, Macmillan, 1967.
8. *Works,* Vol. 12, p. 311.
9. *Works,* Vol. 8, p. 128.
10. *Works,* Vol. 34, p. 547.
11. *Works,* Vol. 8, p. xxxiii.
12. *Works,* Vol. 2, p. 341.
13. *Works,* Vol. 12, p. 380.